KU-015-374

HAMLYN
ALL COLOUR
FOOD FOR KIDS

GOOD FOOD KIDS WILL LOVE

HAMLYN
ALL COLOUR
FOOD FOR KIDS

hamlyn

Note

- Both metric and imperial measurements are given for the recipes. Use one set of measures only, not a mixture of both.

- Ovens should be preheated to the specified temperature. If using a fan-assisted oven, follow the manufacturer's instructions for adjusting the time and temperature. Grills should also be preheated.

- This book includes dishes made with nuts and nut derivatives. It is advisable for those with known allergic reactions to nuts and nut derivatives to avoid dishes made with nuts and nut oils. It is also prudent to check the labels of preprepared ingredients for the possible inclusion of nut derivatives.

- The Department of Health advises that eggs should not be consumed raw. This book contains some dishes made with raw or lightly cooked eggs. It is prudent for more vulnerable people such as pregnant and nursing mothers, invalids, the elderly, babies and very young children to avoid uncooked or lightly cooked dishes made with eggs.

- Meat and poultry should be cooked thoroughly. To test if poultry is cooked, pierce the flesh through the thickest part with a skewer or fork – the juices should run clear, never pink or red.

- Where pepper is listed in the recipe ingredients, always use freshly ground black pepper.

MORAY COUNCIL LIBRARIES & INFO.SERVICES	
20 19 86 92	
Askews	
641.5622	

First published in Great Britain in 2007 by Hamlyn,
a division of Octopus Publishing Group Ltd
2–4 Heron Quays, London E14 4JP

Copyright © Octopus Publishing Group Ltd 2007

All rights reserved. No part of this work may be reproduced or utilized in any form or by any means, electronic or mechanical, including photocopying, recording or by any information storage and retrieval system, without the prior written permission of the publisher.

ISBN-13: 978-0-600-61589-7

ISBN-10: 0-600-61589-8

A CIP catalogue record for this book is available from the British Library

Printed and bound in China

10 9 8 7 6 5 4 3 2 1

While all reasonable care has been taken in the preparation of this book, neither the publishers nor the editors can accept responsibility for any consequences arising from the use of the information provided herein.

Contents

Introduction

These days we are all aware of the importance of a healthy, balanced diet and the positive effects that this can have on our general well-being. Eating habits and attitudes towards food are often developed in early childhood and this means it's very important for toddlers and children to be introduced to a wide range of foods in a fun, relaxed way. Good habits picked up at a young age can last a lifetime and happy mealtime experiences will encourage a healthy interest in food.

Balancing act

A balanced diet doesn't begin and end at the dinner table. The knock-on effects can be seen when it comes to behaviour, concentration at school and sleeping patterns. Fizzy drinks, sugary snacks and fast food are prominent features in many people's diets but it's important to teach children that these foods are occasional treats and not everyday options. They contain empty calories that won't meet the nutritional needs of a growing child. Instead, encourage children to snack on fruit and choose juices and smoothies over carbonated drinks.

It's very important for children to be introduced to a well-balanced diet from a young age. This means they should be eating a wide range of fresh fruit and vegetables, protein and carbohydrates. Try to choose healthier, complex carbohydrates such as wholemeal or granary bread, wholemeal pasta and brown rice and serve desserts such as a simple banana split or fresh fruit salad to encourage children to eat fruit.

Making a meal of it

To encourage an interest in food, why not ask your children to choose some of the family meals? Of course, this will need to be within reason but the more you include children in mealtimes, the more likely they are to really enjoy the food and the occasion. This would make a great weekend activity: choose the meal with the children; go and buy the ingredients; prepare the meal together and then sit down and eat it.

This doesn't mean that home-cooked meals have to be limited to the weekend. Many people reach for ready meals in desperation, as the constraints of busy lives mean time is in short supply. However, fresh, homemade dishes needn't take hours to prepare – a delicious family meal can often be created from scratch in less time than it takes to heat a ready meal in the oven. It's true, you'll need to be a little more organized in terms of shopping and preparation, but why not plan some meals for the week and shop online? Use the time you save by not going to the supermarket to prepare a couple of recipes. If you make double quantities you can freeze batches for a really quick supper on another occasion.

Kids in the kitchen

Children love to get involved in preparing their food and you should encourage them to watch, learn and take part. Obviously this is not always possible so try and set aside a few hours when you have more time to spare and can give them your full attention. There's no better way for children to learn about ingredients and cooking techniques than by making simple recipes themselves. As well as gaining an understanding of the food they eat, cooking will give them a sense of pride and independence and it will provide them with skills they can use all their lives. Kids love being creative and cooking is a chance to channel some of this creative energy. Many of the recipes in this book are ideal for parents and children to prepare together and then sit down and enjoy as a family.

It's a good idea to begin with something really quick and simple and preferably a recipe that doesn't require too much chopping; that way they can do most of the preparation themselves. You will be able to talk about the different ingredients and explain safety in the kitchen as you go along and, of course, the fact that all good cooks leave the kitchen clean and tidy after they've finished! As your children gain in confidence you can move on to more adventurous recipes, or just allow them to help when you're preparing the family meal.

Making food fun

Many children go through a fussy or picky stage with food and it's important to deal with this the right way. After all, eating should be an enjoyable experience and if mealtimes become a battleground then the whole family will suffer. Children can be very wary of trying different things so any new ingredient or meal should be introduced slowly. It may well take a few attempts for something new on the menu to be sampled but just be patient. If a child sees the rest of the family trying different foods they will most likely be intrigued enough to give it a go at some point. Here are a few ideas for stress-free mealtimes:

• Although we might like to see a plate piled high with food, this can be a little daunting for a child. It's better to give a small portion and then encourage your child to ask for more if they are still hungry.

• Liven up dinner plates by making patterns with the food. Vegetables cut into shapes or arranged to make a face can make a meal much more appetizing for a child.

• Try using different coloured foods – this will make the meal look more exciting and might encourage children to try different things.

• Fussy eaters might be encouraged by vegetable or fruit purées accompanied by pitta bread or breadsticks for dipping as an introduction to a new food.

Basic recipes

Most of the recipes in this book are self-contained and can be made without reference to other sections or recipes. However, several of the savoury dishes, including many soups and some meat dishes, use stock, and although it is possible to use granules and cubes, homemade stock has a better depth of flavour and does not contain extra salt or unknown flavourings.

The birthday cakes in the final section can be made with good-quality, shop-bought cakes and decorated as described. However, nothing equals the flavour and texture of homemade cakes. Fairy cakes can be made following recipe 210, and a recipe for a basic Victoria sponge is given below. This basic pancake recipe will also be useful, especially for the breakfast recipes.

Chicken stock

Preparation time: **10 minutes**	**1 large chicken carcass, including any trimmings like the neck, heart and gizzard if available**
Cooking time: **1¹⁄₂–2 hours**	**1 onion, roughly chopped** **1 large carrot, roughly chopped** **several bay leaves**
Makes: **about 1 litre (1³⁄₄ pints)**	**1 teaspoon peppercorns**

Pack the chicken carcass into a large saucepan, crushing the bones if necessary to make it fit. Add the trimmings, vegetables, bay leaves and peppercorns. Just cover with cold water. Bring slowly to the boil, reduce the heat and simmer gently for 1¹⁄₂–2 hours.

Strain through a sieve and leave to cool before chilling or freezing.

Vegetable stock

Preparation time: **10 minutes**	**500 g (1 lb) mixed vegetables (excluding potatoes, parsnips and other starchy root vegetables), chopped**
Cooking time: **about 30 minutes**	**1 garlic clove** **6 peppercorns** **1 bouquet garni**
Makes: **1 litre (1³⁄₄ pints)**	

Put all the ingredients in a large saucepan and add about 1.2 litres (2 pints) water to cover. Bring to the boil and simmer gently for about 30 minutes, removing any scum that rises to the surface.

Strain through a sieve and leave to cool before chilling.

Victoria sandwich cake

Preparation time: **20 minutes, plus cooling**	**175 g (6 oz) unsalted butter, softened** **175 g (6 oz) caster sugar** **3 eggs, beaten**
Cooking time: **25 minutes**	**175 g (6 oz) self-raising flour** **5 tablespoons strawberry or raspberry jam**
Oven temperature: **180°C (350°F), Gas Mark 4**	**icing sugar, glacé icing or buttercream, to decorate**

Serves: **8**

Grease and base-line 2 x 18 cm (7 inch) round sandwich tins. Put the butter and sugar in a bowl and beat well until the ingredients are pale in colour and light and fluffy.

Gradually beat in the eggs, a little at a time, beating well after each addition. Make sure the mixture is thick and smooth before each addition. If it starts to curdle, beat in a spoonful of the flour.

Sift the flour into the bowl, then fold it into the mixture. Don't beat it or overmix, or you'll knock out all the air. Divide the mixture between the tins and level the surface. Bake in a preheated oven, 180°C (350°F), Gas Mark 4, for about 25 minutes or until risen and just firm to the touch.

Pancakes

Preparation time: **15 minutes, plus resting**	**125 g (4 oz) plain flour** **pinch of salt** **1 egg, lightly beaten**
Cooking time: **about 10 minutes**	**300 ml (¹⁄₂ pint) milk** **light olive oil, vegetable oil or butter, for greasing**
Makes: **8–10 pancakes**	

Put the flour and salt in a bowl and make a well in the centre. Pour the egg and a little of the milk into the well. Whisk the liquid, gradually incorporating the flour to make a smooth paste. Whisk in the remaining milk. Allow to rest.

Put a little oil or butter in an 18 cm (7 inch) pancake pan or heavy-based frying pan and heat until it starts to smoke. Pour off the excess oil and pour a little batter into the pan, tilting the pan until the base is coated in a thin layer. (Alternatively, use a small ladle to measure the batter into the pan.) Cook for 1–2 minutes or until the underside is starting to turn golden.

Flip the pancake with a palette knife and cook for a further 30–45 seconds until it is golden on the other side. Slide the pancake out of the pan and make the remaining pancakes, re-oiling the pan as necessary.

1 Breakfasts

1 Boiled eggs with anchovy soldiers

2 Get-up-and-go muesli

Preparation time:
10 minutes

Cooking time:
3–4 minutes

Serves: **4**

8 anchovy fillets in oil, drained
25 g (1 oz) unsalted butter, softened
4 large eggs
4 thick slices of white bread
pepper
salad cress, to serve

Wash the anchovies, pat them dry with kitchen paper and chop finely. Beat them into the butter and season with pepper.

Boil the eggs for 3–4 minutes or until softly set. Meanwhile, toast the bread, butter one side with the anchovy butter and cut into fingers. Serve the eggs with the anchovy toast and some cress.

Preparation time:
5 minutes, plus soaking

Serves: **1**

75 ml (3 fl oz) soya milk
50 g (2 oz) oatmeal, wheat or rye flakes
25 g (1 oz) raisins
50 g (2 oz) natural yogurt
1 apple, grated
juice of 1/2 orange
25 g (1 oz) chopped mixed nuts (such as almonds, walnuts, brazils, hazelnuts and cashews)
25 g (1 oz) wheatgerm
1 teaspoon clear honey
fresh fruit, such as bananas and raspberries (optional)

Put the milk in a bowl and add the cereal flakes and raisins. Cover the bowl and leave the muesli to soak overnight in the refrigerator.

Next morning, stir in the yogurt, apple, orange juice and nuts. Mix in the wheatgerm and drizzle with honey. Top the muesli with fresh fruit, if liked.

COOK'S NOTES Some children may not like anchovies, but others will love them. Try making this dish for your little ones and see if they enjoy the taste.

3 Eggy bread with bananas

4 Wholemeal muffins with scrambled egg

Preparation time:
5 minutes, plus soaking

Cooking time: **15 minutes**

Serves: **4**

4 eggs
3 tablespoons single cream
**1 teaspoon ground cinnamon, plus extra
  to serve**
4 thick slices of wholemeal fruit bread
75 g (3 oz) butter
4 bananas, sliced

TO SERVE:
clear honey or maple syrup
single cream or Greek yogurt (optional)

Preparation time:
5 minutes

Cooking time:
10 minutes

Serves: **2**

2 wholemeal English muffins
butter, for spreading
4 eggs
1 tablespoon flaxseed oil
2 tablespoons soya milk
salt and pepper (optional)
snipped chives, to serve (optional)

Put the eggs, cream and cinnamon in a bowl and beat them with a fork. Pour the mixture into a shallow, flat-bottomed dish, add the bread and leave to soak for 5 minutes. Turn over and soak for a further 5 minutes.

Heat the butter in a nonstick frying pan. When it is foaming, add the bread to the pan and cook for 4–5 minutes on each side or until golden. Put the cooked bread on a heated serving plate and keep warm in a low oven.

Add the bananas to the pan and toss gently for 5 minutes. Spoon the bananas over the bread, drizzle with honey or maple syrup, dust with cinnamon and serve. For an extra treat, add a splash of single cream or Greek yogurt.

Split the muffins and toast them on both sides. Spread them with butter and keep warm in a low oven.

Beat together the eggs, flaxseed oil and soya milk. Pour the mixture into a nonstick saucepan and heat gently, stirring continuously. When the eggs start to look cooked, remove them from the heat and pile on to the hot muffins. Season with a little salt and pepper and garnish with a few snipped chives, if liked.

COOK'S NOTES Muffins can be frozen on the day of purchase and make a good standby ingredient, ready for use in a quick meal, so they are great for a speedy breakfast such as this one.

5 Banana muffins

6 Power pancakes

Preparation time:	**200 g (7 oz) plain white flour**
10 minutes	**3 teaspoons baking powder**
	1¹/₂ teaspoons ground cinnamon
	pinch of grated nutmeg
Cooking time:	**50 g (2 oz) ground almonds**
20–25 minutes	**50 g (2 oz) soft brown sugar**
	2 ripe bananas, about 250 g (8 oz) peeled
Oven temperature:	**weight**
190°C (375°F), Gas Mark 5	**2 eggs**
	2 tablespoons sunflower oil
Makes:	**125 ml (4 fl oz) skimmed milk**
10 muffins	**3 tablespoons clear honey**

Line a muffin tin with 10 paper cases. Sift the flour, baking powder and cinnamon into a bowl and stir in the nutmeg, almonds and sugar.

Lightly mash the bananas and work in the eggs, oil, milk and honey to make a sloppy paste. Combine the banana mixture with the dry ingredients, first using a fork and then with a tablespoon.

Spoon the batter into the paper cases and bake in a preheated oven, 190°C (375°F), Gas Mark 5, for 20–25 minutes or until well risen.

Preparation time:	**50 g (2 oz) rolled oats**
15 minutes	**1 egg**
	75 g (3 oz) cottage cheese
Cooking time:	**¹/₄ teaspoon vanilla extract**
10 minutes	**1 teaspoon peanut or almond butter**
	vegetable oil, for greasing
Serves: **2**	
	FRUIT PURÉE:
	200 g (7 oz) strawberries
	50 ml (2 fl oz) apple juice
	TO SERVE:
	50 g (2 oz) strawberries and raspberries
	2 tablespoons yogurt (optional)
	1 tablespoon chopped nuts (optional)

Put the rolled oats in a food processor or blender and process on high for 1 minute to make flour. Turn into a bowl and add the egg, cottage cheese, vanilla extract and peanut or almond butter. Stir until mixed.

Make the fruit purée by blending the fruit and apple juice together in a food processor.

Lightly oil a heavy-based frying pan, heat and add spoonfuls of the batter mixture to the pan. Cook the pancakes for a few minutes on both sides, re-oiling the pan for each one as necessary.

Pour the fruit purée over the pancakes, scatter with the fresh fruit and add a spoonful of yogurt and a sprinkling of chopped nuts, if liked.

COOK'S NOTES Use any fruit available in season for the purée, such as mango, papaya, blueberries, blackberries or kiwifruit.

7 Pancake stack with maple syrup

8 Mini raspberry pancakes

Preparation time:
10 minutes

Cooking time:
10 minutes

Serves: **4**

1 egg
65 g (2¹/₂ oz) plain white flour
125 ml (4 fl oz) milk
2–3 tablespoons vegetable oil
1 tablespoon sugar
maple syrup, to serve

Put the egg, flour, milk, oil and sugar in a bowl and mix until smooth and creamy.

Heat a large nonstick frying pan over a medium heat and place a ladleful of the batter in each corner to make 4 pancakes. Cook the pancakes for 1–2 minutes or until they start to set and air bubbles rise to the top and burst. Turn over the pancakes and cook on the other side for 1 minute.

Repeat twice more to make 12 small pancakes in all. Bring to the table as a stack, drizzled with maple syrup. Serve 3 pancakes to each person.

Preparation time:
10 minutes

Cooking time:
6–8 minutes

Serves: **4**

200 g (7 oz) self-raising flour
25 g (1 oz) caster sugar
1 teaspoon baking powder
1 teaspoon vanilla extract
2 eggs
250 ml (8 fl oz) milk
sunflower oil, for cooking
butter, for spreading

TO SERVE:
maple syrup
125 g (4 oz) fresh or frozen raspberries

Put the flour, sugar, baking powder, vanilla extract and eggs in a bowl. Gradually whisk in the milk, little by little, until the mixture is smooth and all the milk has been added.

Brush a little oil over the base of a large nonstick frying pan and heat for 1–2 minutes. Add spoonfuls of the pancake mixture to the pan, leaving space between each spoonful to keep the pancakes separate.

Cook the pancakes for 1–2 minutes until they start to set and air bubbles rise to the top and burst. Turn over the pancakes and cook on the other side for 1 minute. Continue making pancakes in the same way until all the mixture is used up.

Spread the pancakes with butter and stack on serving plates. Drizzle with maple syrup and sprinkle with raspberries.

COOK'S NOTES These pancakes also make a great after-dinner treat. Try serving with scoops of vanilla ice cream or fresh fruit.

9 French toast

10 Ricotta griddle cakes

Preparation time:	**1 egg**
5 minutes	**1 tablespoon milk**
	2 slices of fruit bread
Cooking time:	**15 g (¹/₂ oz) butter**
6 minutes	**1 tablespoon sunflower oil**
	1 tablespoon caster sugar
Serves: **1**	**pinch of ground cinnamon (optional)**
	satsuma or orange segments, to serve

Break the egg into a shallow bowl, add the milk and beat together until well mixed.

Cut the bread into strips or triangles. Dip a few pieces of bread into the egg mixture, turning until they are covered.

Lift the bread from the egg mixture, letting the extra mixture drain back into the bowl.

Heat the butter and half the oil in a large, nonstick frying pan and cook the bread for 2–3 minutes, turning once. Dip and cook the rest of the bread in the same way.

Sprinkle with the sugar and add the cinnamon, if liked. Serve with satsuma or orange segments.

Preparation time:	**175 g (6 oz) self-raising flour**
5 minutes	**¹/₂ teaspoon baking powder**
	1 tablespoon caster sugar
Cooking time:	**250 g (8 oz) ricotta cheese**
6 minutes (per batch)	**3 eggs**
	200 ml (7 fl oz) milk
Serves: **4**	**2 tablespoons sunflower oil**
	butter and jam, to serve

Put the flour, baking powder and sugar in a bowl. Add the ricotta, eggs and a little of the milk and whisk together until smooth. Gradually whisk in the remaining milk.

Heat the oil in a heavy-based, nonstick frying pan. Wipe the pan with kitchen paper to remove excess oil. Drop spoonfuls of the mixture into the frying pan and cook for 3–4 minutes or until bubbles form on the top and the cakes are golden-brown underneath. Loosen the cakes and turn them over. Cook the second side for 1–2 minutes or until golden and the cakes are cooked through.

Remove the cakes with a palette knife and keep them hot. Cook the remaining mixture, wiping the griddle or pan with the oily kitchen paper between batches as needed.

Serve the cakes while still hot, spread with butter and jam.

COOK'S NOTES Try a fun variation by cutting shapes from plain white sliced bread with biscuit cutters. To make a savoury version with wholemeal bread, omit the sugar and serve with ketchup.

11 Late great breakfast

Preparation time:	**400 g (13 oz) ready-rolled puff pastry**
15 minutes	**15 g (¹/₂ oz) butter, plus extra for greasing**
	1 red pepper, cored, deseeded and
	chopped
Cooking time:	**2 tomatoes, cut in wedges**
15–20 minutes	**125 g (4 oz) button mushrooms, halved**
	2 tablespoons olive oil
Oven temperature:	**6 eggs**
220°C (425°F), Gas Mark 7	**8 thin-cut rashers of streaky or back**
	bacon
Serves: **4**	**salt**

Unroll the pastry and cut out 4 rectangles, each 12 x 10 cm
(5 x 4 inches). Use the tip of a small knife to make a shallow
cut about 1 cm (¹/₂ inch) in from the edges of each rectangle,
making sure you do not cut right through to the base. Place the
pastry rectangles on a lightly buttered baking sheet.

Arrange the peppers, tomatoes and mushrooms on the pastry cases,
keeping them away from the marked rims. Drizzle with 1 tablespoon of
the oil and bake in a preheated oven, 220°C (425°F), Gas Mark 7, for
15–20 minutes or until the pastry is well risen and golden.

Meanwhile, beat the eggs in a bowl with a pinch of salt. Cut the rind
off the bacon. Heat the remaining oil in a nonstick frying pan and fry
the bacon for about 2 minutes on each side until crisp.

Melt the butter in a small saucepan. Tip in the beaten eggs and cook
over a gentle heat, stirring continuously until scrambled.

Transfer the cooked pastries to 4 serving plates. Spoon some
scrambled eggs on to the centre of each and top with the bacon
rashers. Serve immediately.

12 Waffles with summer berry compote

Preparation time:	**150 g (5 oz) strawberries, quartered**
5 minutes	**150 g (5 oz) raspberries**
	150 g (5 oz) blueberries
Cooking time:	**2 tablespoons elderflower cordial**
5 minutes each waffle	**4 tablespoons low-fat Greek yogurt,**
	to serve
Makes:	
8 waffles	WAFFLES:
	125 ml (4 fl oz) semi-skimmed milk
	2 eggs, separated
	75 g (3 oz) unsalted butter, melted
	125 g (4 oz) wholemeal self-raising flour
	2 tablespoons icing sugar, sifted
	grated rind of ¹/₂ lemon

Put the milk in a bowl. Add the egg yolks and whisk lightly. Add
1 tablespoon of the melted butter to the milk and work in lightly
with a fork.

Sift the flour into a bowl, make a well in the centre of the flour and
gradually beat in the milk and remaining butter. Whisk the egg whites
until they are stiff enough to hold firm peaks, then fold into the batter
with the icing sugar and the lemon rind.

Grease a preheated waffle iron and pour in about one-eighth of the
batter. Close the lid and cook for 4–5 minutes, turning the iron once or
twice if you are using a stove-top model. When the waffle is golden-
brown and properly cooked, cover and keep warm while you cook the
remaining waffles.

Put all the berries and the elderflower cordial in a small saucepan and
heat gently until the berries are just starting to release their juices.

Put 2 waffles on each plate and serve with the berries and a spoonful
of Greek yogurt.

13 Pineapple soya wheatgerm smoothie

14 Cranberry smoothie

Preparation time: **5 minutes**	**125 g (4 oz) pineapple** **500 ml (17 fl oz) soya milk** **2 tablespoons raw wheatgerm**
Serves: **2**	**a few ice cubes** **ground cinnamon, to decorate (optional)**

Chop the pineapple and put into a food processor or blender with the soya milk, wheatgerm and a few ice cubes. Blend until smooth.

Pour the smoothie into tall glasses and sprinkle with ground cinnamon, to decorate, if liked.

Preparation time: **10 minutes, plus cooling**	**50 g (2 oz) cranberries (thawed if frozen)** **3 tablespoons caster sugar** **100 ml (3¹/₂ fl oz) water**
Cooking time: **5 minutes**	**450 ml (³/₄ pint) plain yogurt** **250 ml (8 fl oz) coconut milk**
Serves: **4**	TO SERVE: **cracked ice cubes** **mint sprigs** **gooseberries (or kiwifruit)** **fresh cranberries**

Put the cranberries, sugar and water in a saucepan and heat gently to dissolve the sugar. Bring to the boil and cook for 5 minutes. Remove the pan from the heat and allow to cool completely.

Put the cranberry syrup in a blender or food processor with the yogurt and coconut milk and blend until smooth.

Divide the smoothie among 4 tall glasses filled with cracked ice and serve decorated with a sprig of mint, and with a gooseberry (or a piece of kiwifruit) and a cranberry threaded on to a cocktail stick.

15 Bugsy banana

16 Whacky wizard

Preparation time:
5 minutes

Makes:
200 ml (7 fl oz)

150 g (5 oz) carrot
100 g (3¹/₂ oz) orange
100 g (3¹/₂ oz) banana
1 dried apricot
a few ice cubes

Juice the carrot and orange. Blend in a blender with the banana, apricot and some ice cubes. Decorate with chunks of banana, if liked.

Preparation time:
5 minutes

Makes:
200 ml (7 fl oz)

100 g (3¹/₂ oz) mango
200 g (7 oz) apple
125 g (4 oz) cucumber
a few ice cubes

Juice all of the ingredients and blend with a couple of ice cubes for a fruity slush drink.

COOK'S NOTES Full of iron, calcium and potassium, this non-dairy smoothie is great for bones and teeth and keeping colds at bay. Bananas are also full of tryptophan which is renowned for its calming properties, so this is a good one for excitable children.

COOK'S NOTES Juicing is a good way to gradually introduce vegetables into the diet of fussy children, especially when combined with sweet fruits. Cucumber is extremely hydrating, making this a great cooling drink for active kids.

17 Fruit smoothies

Preparation time:
5 minutes

Serves: **2**

PEACH AND RASPBERRY:
**2 ripe peaches, halved, stoned and
roughly chopped
100 g (3¹/₂ oz) raspberries (thawed
if frozen)
4 tablespoons fromage frais
200 ml (7 fl oz) full-fat milk**

APRICOT:
**411 g (13¹/₂ oz) can apricot halves in
natural juice
100 g (3¹/₂ oz) ricotta cheese**

STRAWBERRY:
**100 g (3¹/₂ oz) strawberries
200 g (7 oz) Greek yogurt
200 ml (7 fl oz) full-fat milk**

Put all of the ingredients for each smoothie in a blender or food
processor and blend until smooth.

Press through a sieve, then pour into glasses. Serve with straws.

18 Pink blush strawberry smoothie

Preparation time:
5 minutes

Serves: **2**

**4 strawberries
1 small ripe banana
1 ripe peach
150 g (5 oz) strawberry yogurt
1 teaspoon clear honey
150 ml (¹/₄ pint) apple or orange juice**

Hull and halve the strawberries, cut the banana into thick slices, and
remove the stone from the peach and slice it thickly. Put all of the fruits
in a blender or food processor and add the yogurt, honey and fruit juice.

Blend together until smooth, then pour into glasses and serve with
straws. Decorate the glass with a strawberry or a peach slice.

COOK'S NOTES For a tropical variation try making this smoothie
with 1 small mango and the juice of 1 lime instead of the peach
and strawberries.

19 Citrus juice

20 Hot carob

Preparation time:
5 minutes

1 carrot, about 125 g (4 oz)
2 oranges, about 200 g (7 oz)

Serves: **1**

Peel the oranges and break them into segments. Juice the oranges with the carrot. Serve immediately.

Preparation time:
5 minutes

Cooking time:
5 minutes

200 ml (7 fl oz) soya milk
2 teaspoons carob powder
1–2 teaspoons clear honey

Serves: **1**

Heat the milk in a saucepan until it is nearly boiling. Add the carob powder and honey and stir or whisk until frothy.

Pour into a mug and serve.

COOK'S NOTES Making your own juice allows you plenty of scope to experiment with flavours. Vary this recipe by adding apple and/or grated fresh root ginger.

2 Fast lunches

21 Sausage and bacon rolls   22 Burger pitta pockets

 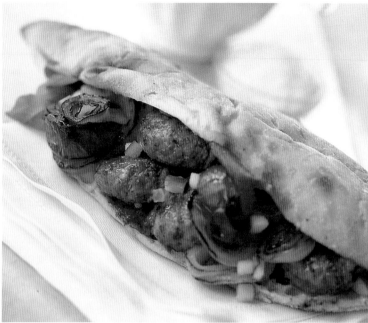

Preparation time:	**8 strips of bacon**
5 minutes	**1–2 teaspoons Dijon mustard**
	4 large beef or pork sausages or
Cooking time:	**frankfurters**
10 minutes	**8 large sage leaves**
	2 tablespoons vegetable oil
Serves: **4**	**4 long bread rolls or frankfurter rolls**
	25 g (1 oz) butter, softened
	relishes, to serve

Stretch each bacon strip with the back of a knife and spread one side of each strip with a little mustard. Wrap 2 strips around each sausage, with the mustard on the inside. Tuck the sage leaves under the bacon and secure with cocktail sticks.

Heat the oil in a large, nonstick frying pan and cook the sausages for 10 minutes over a moderately high heat, shaking the pan occasionally, until the bacon is browned on all sides.

Split the rolls in half lengthways and toast lightly. Spread the cut surfaces with butter and a little mustard, if liked. Remove the cocktail sticks and place one sausage in each roll. Serve immediately with a selection of relishes.

Preparation time:	**40 g (1½ oz) margarine or butter, softened**
15 minutes	**1 tablespoon tomato, corn or chilli relish**
	2 teaspoons corn oil
Cooking time:	**16 mini hamburger patties**
20 minutes	**1 large onion, sliced and separated**
	into rings
Oven temperature:	**4 large pitta breads**
190°C (375°F), Gas Mark 5	**8 cherry tomatoes**
	5 cm (2 inches) cucumber, diced
Makes:	**corn salad, to garnish**
4 pockets	

In a small bowl mix together the margarine or butter and relish and set aside. Heat the oil in a large, nonstick frying pan, add the hamburgers and cook for 3 minutes, turning once. Add the onion rings and fry for 2 minutes. Transfer the hamburgers and onion to a plate.

Make a slit down one side of each pitta bread and open to form a pocket. Spread the margarine and relish mixture inside and over the top. Put all the pittas on a large piece of foil. Add the hamburgers, tomatoes and a few onion rings to each one.

Wrap the foil around the pittas to cover them completely, and place the foil parcel on a baking sheet and cook in a preheated oven, 190°C (375°F), Gas Mark 5, for 10 minutes. Fold back the foil to uncover the tops of the pittas and return to the oven for 5 minutes to crisp up.

Remove the pittas from the oven and add the diced cucumber. Serve immediately, garnished with the corn salad.

COOK'S NOTES These rolls make a great party-time treat for little fingers to hold, and grown-ups will love them too!

23 Quick focaccia pizzas

Preparation time:
10–12 minutes

Cooking time:
5–10 minutes

Oven temperature:
240°C (475°F), Gas Mark 9

Serves: **4–6**

3 roasted red peppers (from a jar), drained and diced
3 sun-dried tomatoes in oil, drained and diced
6 tablespoons grated Parmesan cheese
3 tablespoons finely chopped fresh coriander or flat leaf parsley
2 garlic cloves, finely chopped
75 g (3 oz) pepperoni, chopped
olive oil, for greasing and sprinkling
12 slices of focaccia or ciabatta bread
salt and pepper
basil leaves, to garnish

Combine the peppers, sun-dried tomatoes, half the Parmesan, coriander or parsley, garlic and pepperoni, and season with salt and pepper.

Put the focaccia or ciabatta bread on a lightly oiled baking sheet. Spread a little of the pepper mixture over each piece and sprinkle over the remaining Parmesan and a few drops of olive oil.

Bake in a preheated oven, 240°C (475°F), Gas Mark 9, for 5–10 minutes, until the topping is bubbling. Serve immediately, garnished with basil leaves.

24 BLT sandwich

Preparation time:
5–8 minutes

Cooking time:
5–7 minutes

Makes:
1 sandwich

2 rashers of lean bacon
2 slices of wholemeal or multi-grain bread
2 tablespoons mayonnaise
3 cherry tomatoes, halved
about 4 baby lettuce leaves
salt and pepper

Heat a small, nonstick frying pan and cook the bacon, turning once, until it is golden-brown and crisp. Remove and drain on kitchen paper.

Toast the bread on both sides. Spread one side with mayonnaise and arrange the bacon, tomato and lettuce over one slice. Season with salt and pepper and top with the other piece of toast. Serve hot or cold.

COOK'S NOTES For a change use rye or white bread and put a slice of Cheddar cheese on top of the toast and grill until bubbling, then place the remaining ingredients on top but omit the mayonnaise.

Preparation time: **10–12 minutes**	**6 rashers of bacon** **6 slices of multi-grain bread** **6 tablespoons mayonnaise**
Cooking time: **5–7 minutes**	**8 lettuce leaves** **2 large slices of cooked turkey** **2 tomatoes, sliced thinly**
Makes: **2 sandwiches**	**salt and pepper**

Heat a large, nonstick frying pan and cook the bacon, turning once, for 5–7 minutes until it is golden-brown and crisp. Remove and drain on kitchen paper.

Toast the bread on both sides and spread one side of each slice with 1 tablespoon of mayonnaise. Arrange 2 lettuce leaves on each of 2 slices of toast and sprinkle with salt and pepper to taste.

Arrange a slice of turkey on top of the lettuce on each sandwich, then top with another slice of toast, mayonnaise side up. Arrange the remaining lettuce leaves on top and add the tomato slices, then the crisp bacon, cutting the strips to fit as necessary.

Cover with the remaining 2 slices of toast, mayonnaise side down. Leave the sandwiches whole or cut into 4 triangles and pierce with long cocktail sticks. Serve immediately.

Preparation time: **10 minutes**	**2 small chicken breasts, thinly sliced** **oil, for greasing** **4 tablespoons hoisin sauce**
Cooking time: **8 minutes**	**2 large wheat tortillas** **2 tablespoons sesame seeds** **1 celery stick, shredded**
Serves: **2**	**4 spring onions, trimmed and shredded** **10 cm (4 inch) cucumber, shredded** **1 carrot, grated**

Place the chicken on a lightly oiled, foil-lined grill rack. Cook under a moderate grill for 3–4 minutes on each side until cooked through.

Spread the hoisin sauce over the tortillas to within 2.5 cm (1 inch) of the edges. Arrange the chicken slices down the centre and sprinkle with the sesame seeds and prepared vegetables. Roll up the tortillas to enclose the filling and serve.

COOK'S NOTES This is an ideal recipe for using up chicken from a roast. Roast pork and lamb are also suitable. These filled tortillas are perfect picnic food. Wrap them in napkins for easy eating.

Preparation time:
15 minutes

Serves: **2**

2 slices of bread
butter or margarine, for spreading
a little yeast extract (optional)
2 thin slices of Cheddar cheese
¼ cucumber
1 carrot, cut into long, thin slices
1 cherry tomato, halved
a little salad cress

Cut each slice of bread roughly into the shape of a train, including the driver's cab. Spread lightly with butter or margarine and yeast extract (if used), then cover each 'engine' with a slice of cheese, trimming to fit. Place each train on a serving plate.

Cut 6 slices of cucumber for the wheels and shape 2 funnels and 2 driver's cabs from carrot slices. Cut 2 wedges of cucumber for the cab roofs. Position these and put a halved tomato on each engine.

Add the carrot strips to the engines and add a trail of snipped cress for 'smoke'.

COOK'S NOTES Make an ordinary sandwich more appealing by presenting it as a child's favourite toy. With a little imagination you could make a cruise ship, rocket, car or doll's pram as easily as this train.

Preparation time:
20 minutes, plus infusing and making the pancakes

Cooking time:
30 minutes

Oven temperature:
200°C (400°F), Gas Mark 6

Serves: **4**

pancakes (see basic recipes)
50 g (2 oz) Gruyère cheese, grated
300 g (10 oz) sliced ham
oil, for greasing

BÉCHAMEL SAUCE:
200 ml (7 fl oz) milk
2 bay leaves
1 small onion, quartered
1 teaspoon black peppercorns
50 g (2 oz) butter
40 g (1½ oz) plain flour
300 ml (½ pint) single cream
grated nutmeg
salt and pepper

Make the pancakes and allow them to cool while you make the filling.

Make the sauce. Put the milk in a saucepan with the bay leaves, onion and peppercorns. Bring almost to the boil, remove from the heat and leave to infuse for 15 minutes. Strain through a sieve. Melt the butter in a heavy-based saucepan. Tip in the flour and stir in quickly. Cook gently for 1 minute. Remove from the heat and stir in the strained milk, then the cream. Return to the heat and cook gently, stirring, until the sauce is thick and smooth. Season to taste with nutmeg and salt and pepper.

Remove the pan from the heat and beat the grated cheese into the sauce. Leave the sauce to cool.

Divide the ham and cheese sauce among the pancakes, roll them up and arrange them in a shallow, lightly greased, ovenproof dish. Bake in a preheated oven, 200°C (400°F), Gas Mark 6, for 15 minutes. Serve hot.

Preparation time:
20 minutes, plus chilling

Cooking time:
55–60 minutes

Oven temperature:
**200°C (400°F), Gas Mark 6,
then 180°C (350°F), Gas
Mark 4**

Serves: **4–6**

**175 g (6 oz) shortcrust pastry (thawed if
frozen)
175 g (6 oz) rindless smoked back bacon
250 ml (8 fl oz) single cream
2 eggs, beaten
grated nutmeg
salt and pepper**

Preparation time:
10 minutes

Cooking time:
2–4 minutes

Serves: **1**

**2 small, soft, flour tortillas
2 teaspoons sun-dried tomato paste
1 tomato, sliced
75 g (3 oz) mozzarella cheese, thinly
sliced
few basil leaves, plus extra to garnish
4–6 young spinach leaves
1 tablespoon olive oil
salt and pepper
salad, to serve**

Roll out the pastry on a lightly floured board and line a 20 cm (8 inch) tart tin. Chill the pastry case for 30 minutes, then bake blind in a preheated oven, 200°C (400°F), Gas Mark 6, for 15 minutes. Remove the paper and beans or foil and return the pastry case to the oven for a further 10 minutes.

Meanwhile, make the filling. Grill the bacon until it is crisp, drain it on kitchen paper and crumble or cut it into pieces. Beat the cream and eggs in a bowl with the grated nutmeg and season to taste with salt and pepper. Sprinkle the bacon over the case and pour the cream and egg filling over the top.

Put the tart tin on a baking sheet and bake in a preheated oven, 180°C (350°F), Gas Mark 4, for 30–35 minutes or until the filling is just set and the pastry is golden-brown. Serve warm or cold.

Rinse the tortillas with water to soften them a little, so they will fold and stick together.

Spread the tomato paste over half of each tortilla and arrange the tomato and mozzarella slices on top. Add the basil leaves and spinach and season with salt and pepper.

Fold each tortilla over the filling and press the edges together. (Don't worry if the edges do not stick in places.) Heat the oil in a nonstick frying pan, add the tortillas and fry for 1–2 minutes on each side, until golden. Serve immediately with a salad.

COOK'S NOTES Try grated or sliced Cheddar cheese, chopped ham and mushrooms or your own favourite pizza topping combination.

31 Pasta and bean soup

32 Tomato, garlic and herb loaf

Preparation time:
20 minutes, plus standing

Cooking time:
3 hours 50 minutes

Oven temperature:
180°C (350°F), Gas Mark 4

Serves: **4**

250 g (8 oz) dried haricot beans
2 tablespoons vegetable oil
1 large onion, chopped
2 garlic cloves, crushed
125 g (4 oz) bacon, finely chopped
   (optional)
600 ml (1 pint) vegetable stock
3 tablespoons tomato purée
125 g (4 oz) short-cut macaroni
2 tablespoons finely chopped parsley
1 teaspoon finely chopped basil

TO SERVE:
grated Cheddar or Parmesan cheese
green salad
wholemeal bread

Put the beans in a saucepan, cover with cold water, bring to the boil and boil for 2 minutes. Remove the pan from the heat and leave to stand for 2 hours.

Heat the oil in a nonstick frying pan, add the onion, garlic and bacon (if used) and cook for about 5 minutes or until the onion has softened.

Drain the beans and transfer them to a large saucepan. Add the onion and bacon mixture, pour in the stock and stir in the tomato purée. Bring to the boil, then pour the soup into a casserole dish.

Transfer the covered casserole to a preheated oven, 180°C (350°F), Gas Mark 4, and cook for about 3 hours. Remove the casserole from the oven and purée half the soup in a food processor or blender. Stir the puréed soup back into the casserole, add the macaroni, parsley and basil and cook for another 45 minutes. Serve with a little grated cheese, a side salad and some crusty wholemeal bread.

Preparation time:
15 minutes

Cooking time:
20–25 minutes

Oven temperature:
180°C (350°F), Gas Mark 4

Serves: **4–8**

1 small wholemeal or white wholegrain
   French stick
3 tablespoons extra virgin olive oil
2 tablespoons tomato purée
3 garlic cloves, crushed
2 tablespoons finely chopped parsley

Make deep diagonal cuts in the French stick every 4 cm (1½ inches), cutting almost but not quite through the loaf.

In a bowl mix together the olive oil, tomato purée, garlic and parsley.

Fill each cut in the loaf with a generous spoonful of the garlic mixture, making sure that both sides are evenly coated. Wrap the loaf in foil and bake in a preheated oven, 180°C (350°F), Gas Mark 4, for 20–25 minutes. Serve warm.

COOK'S NOTES The loaf can be wrapped in foil and frozen at the pre-baking stage. Defrost at room temperature for 1 hour and cook as described. It can be frozen for up to 6 months.

33 Sweet and sour salad

Preparation time:
15 minutes

Serves: **2–3**

1 avocado, stoned, peeled and cubed
1 mango, stoned, peeled and cubed
1 papaya, peeled, deseeded and cubed
175 g (6 oz) cooked peeled prawns
200 g (7 oz) cherry tomatoes, halved
2 tablespoons olive or flaxseed oil
juice of 1 lime
handful of snipped chives
salt and pepper (optional)
wholemeal bread, to serve

In a bowl combine the avocado with the mango, papaya, prawns and cherry tomatoes.

Drizzle over the oil and lime juice and add a little salt and pepper (if used). Toss the salad to mix and sprinkle with the chives. Serve with wholemeal bread.

COOK'S NOTES This salad tastes just as good without the prawns, so leave them out if your children prefer.

34 Monstermunch salad

Preparation time:
15 minutes

Serves: **4–6**

2 tablespoons lemon juice
1 tablespoon chopped tarragon (optional)
3 tablespoons mayonnaise
1 teaspoon clear honey or maple syrup
1 cos lettuce
1 carrot, grated
¼ cucumber, diced
200 g (7 oz) can tuna or salmon in water or oil, drained
200 g (7 oz) can cannellini or red kidney beans, drained
3 eggs, hard-boiled, shelled and thickly sliced
salt and pepper

In a small bowl mix together the lemon juice, tarragon (if used), mayonnaise and honey or syrup with a little salt and pepper.

Separate the lettuce leaves, discarding the coarse outer leaves. Wash and drain the lettuce, tear it into pieces and put them in a large salad bowl. Drizzle the dressing over the lettuce and toss together. Add the carrot and cucumber.

Break the tuna or salmon into pieces with a fork. Add the fish and beans to the salad bowl and mix gently. Arrange the slices of egg on top of the salad and serve.

Preparation time: 8 minutes	**4 thick slices of French country bread** **25 g (1 oz) butter, melted** **25 g (1 oz) Parmesan cheese, finely**
Cooking time: 4–5 minutes	**grated** **2 large slices of country-style roast ham** **125 g (4 oz) Emmental or similar Swiss**
Serves: **2**	**cheese, coarsely grated**

Brush one side of each slice of bread with the melted butter and sprinkle with the Parmesan. With the Parmesan-coated sides on the outside, lay down two slices of bread and top each with a slice of ham and half the coarsely grated Emmental.

Top with the remaining two slices of bread and toast in a sandwich grill for 4–5 minutes, or according to the manufacturer's instructions, until the bread is golden and crispy and the Emmental is beginning to ooze from the sides. Serve immediately.

Preparation time: 15 minutes	**1 baking potato, about 250 g (8 oz), peeled** **and scrubbed** **1/2 parsnip, about 150 g (5 oz)**
Cooking time: about 30 minutes	**2 small carrots, about 150 g (5 oz) in total** **3 tablespoons olive oil** **pinch of turmeric**
Oven temperature: 220°C (425°F), Gas Mark 7	**pinch of paprika** **2 eggs** **tomato ketchup, to serve**
Serves: **2**	

Cut the potato and parsnip into wedge-shaped chips, about 6 cm (2¹/₂ inches) long. Cut the carrots into thick sticks, about the same length. Cook in a pan of boiling water for 4 minutes.

Meanwhile, heat the oil in a small roasting tin in a preheated oven, 220°C (425°F), Gas Mark 7, for 2 minutes.

Drain the vegetables, add them to the hot oil and toss to coat. Sprinkle with the spices and roast in the oven for 20 minutes. Turn the vegetables and make a space in the middle of them. Break the eggs into the space and bake for a further 5 minutes or until the eggs are well cooked. Transfer to serving plates and serve with tomato ketchup.

COOK'S NOTES The grated Parmesan coating gives the toast an irresistible crunch. Top it with a perfect fried egg to make a brunch croque madame.

37 Tomato clowns

38 Miss Mouse egg

Preparation time:
15 minutes

Cooking time:
12–13 minutes

Oven temperature:
200°C (400°F), Gas Mark 6

Serves: **2**

2 large tomatoes
1 teaspoon pesto
4 mini mozzarella cheeses, well drained
2 pitted black olives, halved
1 teaspoon olive oil
200 ml (7 fl oz) water
50 g (2 oz) polenta
15 g (½ oz) butter
2 tablespoons full-fat milk
1 small carrot, cut into thin sticks
2 red pepper slices, cut from the base
salt and pepper

Halve the tomatoes crossways and scoop out the cores and seeds. Turn the tomato halves upside down to drain.

Put the tomatoes, cut side up, in a small heatproof dish. Spoon a tiny amount of pesto into each one, add a mini mozzarella and an olive half. Drizzle with oil and bake in a preheated oven, 200°C (400°F), Gas Mark 6, for 10 minutes.

When the tomatoes are almost ready, bring the water to the boil in a small nonstick saucepan. Add the polenta in a steady stream, stirring, then cook, stirring constantly, for 2–3 minutes or until thickened and smooth. Take off the heat and stir in the butter and milk. Season with salt and pepper to taste.

Spoon the soft polenta on to 2 plates. Add the baked tomato eyes and position carrot sticks for eyelashes. Place a small red pepper ring on each face with a sliver of carrot in the centre to resemble a mouth. Serve immediately.

Preparation time:
15 minutes

Serves: **2**

2 eggs, hard-boiled and shelled
2 teaspoons mayonnaise
1 small carrot, coarsely grated
½ red pepper
a little tomato ketchup
15 g (½ oz) medium Cheddar cheese, cubed

Cut a lengthways slice from each egg to reveal the yolk. Scoop out the yolk, mix with the mayonnaise and spoon back into the egg white cases. (The slices are not needed.)

Form the grated carrot into nests on 2 serving plates. Put the eggs, stuffed-side down, on top. Add a red pepper slice for each tail, tiny pepper strips for whiskers and small triangles for ears, positioning these by making tiny slits in the egg white.

Pipe on tomato ketchup eyes and put a cube of cheese in each nest – for the mice to munch on!

COOK'S NOTES Make sailing boats by positioning the eggs, cut side uppermost, on a sea of grated carrot. Cut triangular slices of cheese for sails. Rest these against cocktail stick masts, adding a red pepper or carrot flag to the top of the mast.

39 Cheesy blinis

40 Pizza quiches

Preparation time:
15 minutes

Cooking time:
10–12 minutes

Serves: **4**

BLINIS:
100 g (3¹/2 oz) self-raising flour
¹/2 teaspoon baking powder
75 g (3 oz) medium Cheddar cheese, grated
1 egg
150 ml (¹/4 pint) full-fat milk
oil, for greasing
butter, for spreading

SALAD:
50 g (2 oz) frozen sweetcorn, just defrosted
2 tomatoes, finely chopped
5 cm (2 inch) cucumber, diced
75 g (3 oz) cooked or drained canned red kidney beans

In a bowl toss together all the salad ingredients and set aside.

Make the blinis. Put the flour, baking powder and cheese in a bowl, add the egg and gradually whisk in the milk to make a smooth batter.

Heat a little oil over medium heat in a large, nonstick frying pan. Cook the blinis in batches, dropping dessertspoonfuls of the batter into the pan and spacing them well apart. Cook for 2 minutes or until the top is bubbling and the underside is golden. Turn over and cook until the other side is browned.

Wrap the blinis in a clean napkin to keep warm. Cook the rest of them in the same way, brushing the pan with extra oil as needed.

Serve the blinis warm, spread lightly with butter and accompanied by the fresh salad.

Preparation time:
10 minutes

Cooking time:
20 minutes

Oven temperature:
200°C (400°F), Gas Mark 6

Makes:
6 quiches

500 g (1 lb) puff pastry (thawed if frozen)
3 tablespoons sun-dried tomato paste
375 g (12 oz) cherry tomatoes, halved
50 g (2 oz) pepperoni, thinly sliced
125 g (4 oz) mozzarella cheese, thinly sliced
1 tablespoon olive oil, plus extra for greasing

Thinly roll out the pastry on a lightly floured surface and cut out 6 circles, each 10 cm (4 inch) across. Transfer them to a lightly oiled baking sheet.

Spread tomato paste over the pastry to within 1 cm (¹/2 inch) of the edges. Pile the cherry tomatoes, pepperoni and mozzarella on top.

Drizzle the oil over the top and bake in a preheated oven, 200°C (400°F), Gas Mark 6, for 20 minutes or until the pastry is well risen and golden and the cheese has melted. Serve warm.

41 Stripy cheese on toast   42 Dinner jackets

Preparation time:	**2 slices of bread**
10 minutes	**butter, for spreading**
	75 g (3 oz) Cheddar cheese
Cooking time:	**75 g (3 oz) red Leicester cheese**
10 minutes	
	TO SERVE (OPTIONAL):
Serves: **2**	**halved cherry tomatoes**
	cubes of cucumber

Preheat the grill and lightly toast the bread on both sides. Lightly butter the toast.

Cut the cheese into strips, about 5 mm ($^1/_4$ inch) thick and 2 cm ($^3/_4$ inch) wide. Cover the toast with strips of different yellow and red cheese, alternating the colours.

Put the toast back under the grill and cook until the cheese is bubbling. Serve immediately with halved cherry tomatoes and cubes of cucumber, if using.

Preparation time:	**4 baking potatoes, each about 200 g (7 oz)**
10 minutes	**200 g (7 oz) can tuna, in water or oil, drained**
Cooking time:	**$^1/_2$ red pepper, deseeded and diced**
1$^1/_4$ hours	**1 small dessert apple, cored and diced**
	75 g (3 oz) sweetcorn (thawed if frozen)
Oven temperature:	**3 tablespoons mayonnaise**
200°C (400°F), Gas Mark 6	**3 tablespoons natural yogurt**
	salt and pepper
Serves: **4**	

Scrub the potatoes and prick them with a fork. Bake in a preheated oven, 200°C (400°F), Gas Mark 6, for 1$^1/_4$ hours or until soft. Alternatively, cook in a microwave on a piece of kitchen paper for about 10 minutes or according to the manufacturer's instructions.

Meanwhile, make the filling. Tip the tuna into the bowl and break it into pieces. Add the red pepper and apple to the tuna with the sweetcorn, mayonnaise, yogurt and a little salt and pepper. Mix together with the spoon.

Cut the cooked potatoes in half or cut a cross in the top. Put the potatoes on to plates and spoon the tuna mixture over the top. Serve immediately.

43 Spicy tortillas

44 Pizza mania

Preparation time:
15 minutes

Cooking time:
about 1 hour

Serves: **4**

1 tablespoon olive oil
500 g (1 lb) extra lean minced beef
1 onion, chopped
2 carrots, diced
2 garlic cloves, crushed
2 teaspoons mild paprika
1 teaspoon ground cumin
415 g (13¹/₂ oz) can baked beans
400 g (13 oz) can chopped tomatoes
200 ml (7 fl oz) chicken or beef stock
125 g (4 oz) mixed frozen vegetables
125 g (4 oz) tortilla chips
75 g (3 oz) Cheddar or mozzarella cheese,
  grated
salt and pepper

Heat the oil in a large, nonstick frying pan and add the mince, onion, carrots and garlic. Fry, stirring, until the mince is evenly browned.

Stir in the paprika and cumin and cook for 1 minute. Add the baked beans, tomatoes, stock and salt and pepper.

Bring to the boil, breaking up any large pieces of mince with the spoon. Cover and cook gently for 45 minutes, stirring from time to time.

When the mince is cooked, put the frozen vegetables in a small saucepan, cover with cold water, bring to the boil and cook for 4 minutes. Drain thoroughly.

Transfer the mince mixture to a shallow heatproof dish. Sprinkle the vegetables over and top with the tortilla chips and cheese. Cook under a preheated grill for 2–3 minutes or until the cheese is bubbling and serve immediately.

Preparation time:
15 minutes, plus proving

Cooking time:
8–10 minutes

Oven temperature:
220°C (425°F), Gas Mark 7

Makes:
4 pizzas

375 g (12 oz) strong white bread flour,
  plus extra for kneading
1 teaspoon fast-action dried yeast
1 teaspoon caster sugar
250 ml (8 fl oz) lukewarm water
salt and pepper
salad, to serve

TOPPING:
200 g (7 oz) pizza sauce or passata
  topping
75 g (3 oz) courgette, cubed
50 g (2 oz) sweetcorn (thawed if frozen)
40 g (1¹/₂ oz) thinly sliced salami or ham,
  cut into strips
150 g (5 oz) mozzarella cheese, drained
  and thinly sliced
2 teaspoons pesto sauce or a few basil
  leaves
few pitted olives (optional)

In a large bowl mix together the flour, yeast and sugar. Add some salt and pepper. Gradually mix in the water to make a soft but not sticky dough. Knead the dough on a lightly floured surface for 10 minutes or until it is smooth and elastic.

Cut the dough into 4 pieces and roll each into a rough circle, about 18 cm (7 inches) across. Put them on ungreased baking sheets.

Spread each circle with the pizza sauce or passata. Sprinkle the courgette and sweetcorn over the pizzas and arrange the salami or ham and cheese on top. Dot the pesto over the cheese or add the basil leaves. Add the olives (if used).

Leave the pizzas to rise in a warm place for 30 minutes or until the bread is puffy around the edges. Bake in a preheated oven, 220°C (425°F), Gas Mark 7, for 8–10 minutes or until the edges are golden.

45 Guacamole

46 Cashew dip with veggie dunkers

Preparation time:
10 minutes, plus chilling

Makes:
about 500 ml (17 fl oz)

2 large avocados, stoned and peeled
4 tablespoons lime or lemon juice
1 garlic clove, crushed
1 tablespoon finely chopped onion
1 large tomato, skinned, deseeded and finely chopped
1–2 green chillies, deseeded and finely chopped
1 tablespoon finely chopped fresh coriander leaves
pinch of sugar
salt and pepper
coriander sprigs, to garnish

Put the avocado flesh in a bowl with the lime or lemon juice and mash it with a fork to make a textured paste. Stir in the garlic, onion, tomato, chillies, coriander and sugar. Season with salt and pepper and add some extra lime or lemon juice, if required.

Spoon the mixture into a serving bowl and garnish with coriander sprigs. Cover with clingfilm to help prevent discoloration and chill until required.

Preparation time:
15 minutes

Cooking time:
1–2 minutes

Serves: **4**

100 g (3¹/₂ oz) cashew nuts
200 ml (7 fl oz) Greek or natural yogurt
1 spring onion, trimmed and thinly sliced
2 teaspoons olive oil
little paprika
salt and pepper

TO SERVE:
2 carrots, cut into strips
¹/₄ cucumber, cut into strips
few breadsticks (optional)

Put the nuts in a foil-lined grill pan and cook until lightly browned. Tip them into a blender, food processor or spice mill and grind until they form a fine powder.

Mix the nuts into the yogurt. Stir the spring onion into the mixture and add salt and pepper to taste.

Transfer the dip to a small bowl, drizzle over the olive oil and sprinkle with paprika.

Arrange the carrot and cucumber sticks around the bowl and serve breadsticks, if liked, for dipping.

COOK'S NOTES Don't purée the avocado flesh in a food processor or blender because it will make the texture too smooth. This thick, creamy avocado purée can be used as a dip for crudités or tortilla chips or eaten Mexican-style with tortillas. It can also be used as a sauce for fish and chicken.

47 Zippidy dip with crudités   48 Pumpkin fondue

Preparation time:
15 minutes

Serves: **4**

2 large avocados, stoned and peeled
3 tomatoes, skinned, deseeded and
** chopped**
1 garlic clove, crushed
4 tablespoons lime or lemon juice
1 tablespoon chopped fresh coriander
** leaves**
1/4 teaspoon ground cumin
1/4 teaspoon vegetable bouillon powder
crudités, to serve

Put the avocado flesh in a bowl and mash with a fork until smooth. Add the tomatoes, garlic, lime or lemon juice, coriander, cumin and bouillon powder and mix well to make a chunky dip. Alternatively, for a smoother dip, put all the ingredients in a food processor and blend for 30 seconds.

Serve the dip with an assortment of crudités, such as celery and carrot sticks, apple slices and red pepper strips, or with rice cakes or oatcakes, or spread it on wholemeal toast.

COOK'S NOTES For a variation on this dip mix the avocado with 1 grated apple, 4 tablespoons lemon juice, 50 ml (2 fl oz) apple juice and a handful of toasted sunflower seeds.

Preparation time:
30 minutes

Cooking time:
about 40 minutes

Oven temperature:
180°C (350°F), Gas Mark 4

Serves: **4–6**

2 small pumpkins
2 tablespoons olive oil
1/2 bunch of spring onions, trimmed and
** finely sliced**
1 clove garlic, crushed
250 g (8 oz) Emmental cheese, grated
250 g (8 oz) Gruyère cheese, grated
200 ml (7 fl oz) vegetable stock
1 tablespoon cornflour, mixed to a
** smooth paste with a little water**
grated nutmeg
paprika
a few dried chilli flakes (optional)
salt and pepper

TO SERVE:
apple slices
celery sticks
cubes of bread

Cut a slice off the top of each pumpkin and scoop out the seeds. Scoop out some of the flesh to leave shells with walls about 1 cm (1/2 inch) thick. Brush the inside of each pumpkin with 2 teaspoons oil, put on a baking sheet and bake, with the lid back in position, in a preheated oven, 180°C (350°F), Gas Mark 4, for 30 minutes.

Heat the remaining oil in a saucepan, add most of the spring onions and all the garlic and cook for 2–3 minutes or until softened. Add the cheeses, stock and cornflour paste. Season with salt, pepper and a little grated nutmeg. Heat gently, stirring, until the cheese has melted into a smooth sauce.

Pour the fondue into the baked pumpkins and sprinkle with the remaining spring onions and a little paprika and chilli flakes (if used). Serve with apple, celery and cubed bread for dunking.

3   Lunchbox

49 Peking wraps

50 Spicy chorizo wrap

Preparation time: **10 minutes**	**1 duck breast, about 175 g (6 oz), with skin** **¹/₂ teaspoon Chinese five spice powder**
Cooking time: **about 10 minutes**	**1 tablespoon vegetable oil** **2 large, soft, flour tortillas** **2 tablespoons hoisin sauce**
Makes: **2 wraps**	**2 iceberg lettuce leaves, shredded** **5 cm (2 inch) cucumber, cut into strips** **2 spring onions, trimmed and finely sliced diagonally**

Pat the duck dry on kitchen paper and cut it into thin slices. Put them on a plate and sprinkle with the five spice powder, turning the slices so that they are coated.

Heat the oil in a small, nonstick frying pan and gently cook the duck, turning, for 5 minutes. Transfer the duck to a clean plate.

Warm the tortillas under a hot grill or in a clean frying pan for 1 minute. Alternatively, heat them one at a time in a microwave on full power for 8 seconds or according to the manufacturer's instructions.

Spread hoisin sauce over one side of each tortilla. Scatter a line of lettuce, then the cucumber, spring onions and duck in the centre of each tortilla, keeping the ingredients away from the ends. Fold 2 sides of each tortilla over the ends of the filling and roll them up tightly from an unfolded side so the filling is completely enclosed. Cut the tortillas in half, cover tightly and chill until needed.

Preparation time: **15 minutes**	**2 eggs, beaten** **¹/₄ teaspoon mild chilli powder** **25 g (1 oz) sliced chorizo sausage, shredded**
Cooking time: **5–7 minutes**	**1 tablespoon olive oil** **1 large, soft, flour tortilla**
Makes: **1 wrap**	**1 tablespoon red pesto** **¹/₂ punnet mustard and cress, washed and drained**

Mix together the eggs and chilli powder. Stir in the chorizo.

Heat the oil in a small, nonstick frying pan and add the egg mixture. When the eggs start to set around the edges, push the cooked parts into the centre so the uncooked egg flows to the edges. Cook until the eggs are no longer runny, then let the omelette cook for 3–5 minutes or until just set. Slide the omelette on to a plate and leave to cool.

Warm the tortilla under a hot grill or in a clean frying pan for 1 minute. Alternatively, heat it in a microwave on full power for 8 seconds or according to the manufacturer's instructions.

Spread one side of the tortilla with the pesto and lay the omelette on top. Scatter with the mustard and cress. Fold 2 sides of the tortilla over the ends of the filling and then roll it up tightly from an unfolded side so the filling is completely enclosed. Cut the wrap in half, cover tightly and chill until needed.

COOK'S NOTES These fabulous 'rolled-up sandwiches' are great for picnics or any day you're out and about with your children. You could use a large chicken breast instead of the duck. Cook it for the same time as the duck, then cool and thoroughly chill it before wrapping.

51 Picnic pies

52 Pepper and cheese puffs

Preparation time:	PASTRY:
15 minutes	**100 g (3¹/₂ oz) plain white flour, plus extra for dusting**
Cooking time:	**100 g (3¹/₂ oz) wholemeal flour**
20–25 minutes	**50 g (2 oz) margarine, diced**
	50 g (2 oz) white vegetable shortening, diced
Oven temperature:	**3–4 tablespoons cold water**
180°C (350°F), Gas Mark 4	
Makes:	FILLING:
12 pies	**100 g (3¹/₂ oz) medium Cheddar cheese, grated**
	2 tomatoes, thinly sliced
	3 eggs
	300 ml (¹/₂ pint) full-fat milk
	salt and pepper

Put the flours in a bowl, add the fats and rub in with fingertips until the mixture resembles fine breadcrumbs. Add enough water to mix to a smooth dough. Turn out on a lightly floured surface and knead briefly.

Roll out the dough thinly on a lightly floured surface and cut out 12 rounds, each 10 cm (4 inch) across. Use the dough to line a lightly oiled, 12-section muffin tin, gently pressing the pastry into the edges. Re-roll the trimmings and cut more rounds as needed.

Divide two-thirds of the cheese among the pastry cases. Add the sliced tomatoes, halving them to fit if necessary.

Beat the eggs and milk together with a little seasoning. Pour into the cases and sprinkle over the remaining cheese. Bake in a preheated oven, 180°C (350°F), Gas Mark 4, for 20–25 minutes or until golden and the filling is set. Serve warm or cold.

Preparation time:	**500 g (1 lb) puff pastry (thawed if frozen)**
15 minutes	**flour, for dusting**
	beaten egg, to glaze
Cooking time:	**250 g (8 oz) jar mixed peppers in olive oil**
20 minutes	**400 g (13 oz) can borlotti or cannellini beans, rinsed and drained**
Oven temperature:	**125 g (4 oz) mozzarella cheese, thinly sliced**
200°C (400°F), Gas Mark 6	**50 g (2 oz) Parmesan cheese, grated**
Makes:	**salt and pepper**
8 pies	

Roll out the pastry on a lightly floured surface to a 33 cm (13 inch) square. Cut into 4 squares, then halve each square to make 8 rectangles. Lightly brush the edges with beaten egg.

Divide the peppers among the rectangles, keeping them to one half of each rectangle and at least 1 cm (¹/₂ inch) in from the edges. Scatter the beans over the peppers, then top with the cheeses. Season lightly with salt and pepper.

Fold the other half of each pastry rectangle over the filling and press the edges together firmly to seal. Brush the tops with beaten egg and score lightly with a knife. Transfer to a baking sheet and bake in a preheated oven, 200°C (400°F), Gas Mark 6, for 20 minutes or until risen and golden. Serve warm or cold.

COOK'S NOTES These little pies are equally suitable for picnics and lunchboxes. For older children and adults you could add some chopped olives, garlic, chilli sauce or anchovies to the filling.

53 Sweetcorn and bacon muffins

Preparation time:
10 minutes

Cooking time:
20–25 minutes

Oven temperature:
220°C (425°F), Gas Mark 7

Makes:
12 muffins

200 g (7 oz) frozen sweetcorn
4 rashers of lean bacon, rinded and finely chopped
150 g (5 oz) cornmeal
150 g (5 oz) white self-raising flour
2 teaspoons baking powder
50 g (2 oz) mature Cheddar cheese, grated
4 spring onions, trimmed and finely chopped
200 ml (7 fl oz) semi-skimmed milk
2 eggs
1 tablespoon grainy mustard
2 tablespoons light olive oil, plus extra for greasing

Cook the sweetcorn in boiling water for 2 minutes, drain and rinse under cold running water.

Heat a small, nonstick frying pan and dry-fry the bacon over a moderate heat for about 3 minutes until turning crisp.

Put the cornmeal, flour, baking powder, cheese and spring onions in a mixing bowl. Add the fried bacon pieces.

In another bowl beat together the milk, eggs, mustard and oil until evenly blended. Add to the flour mixture and stir to combine. Spoon the mixture into a lightly oiled 12-section muffin tin and bake in a preheated oven, 220°C (425°F), Gas Mark 7, for 15–20 minutes or until just firm. Loosen the edges of the muffins with a palette knife and transfer to a wire rack to cool. Serve warm or cold.

54 Cheesy corn muffins

Preparation time:
10 minutes

Cooking time:
15 minutes

Oven temperature:
200°C (400°F), Gas Mark 6

Makes:
12 muffins

125 g (4 oz) quick-cook polenta
175 g (6 oz) self-raising flour
2 teaspoons baking powder
100 g (3 1/2 oz) mature Cheddar cheese, grated
150 ml (1/4 pint) milk
2 eggs
2 teaspoons Dijon mustard
4 tablespoons sunflower oil
salt and pepper
butter, to serve

Put the polenta, flour and baking powder in a mixing bowl, then stir in the cheese.

Put the milk, eggs, mustard and oil in a small bowl, add a little salt and pepper and beat together lightly with a fork. Add the milk mixture to the polenta mixture and stir until just mixed.

Line a 12-section muffin tin with paper cases and spoon the muffin mixture into the cases. Bake in a preheated oven, 200°C (400°F), Gas Mark 6, for 15 minutes or until the muffins are well risen and golden-brown. Loosen the edges of the paper cases with a round-bladed knife and transfer to a wire rack. Serve the muffins warm, broken and spread with butter. They are best eaten on the day they are made.

55 Cheese and courgette muffins

56 Feta dip

Preparation time:
10 minutes

Cooking time:
18–20 minutes

Oven temperature:
200°C (400°F), Gas Mark 6

Makes:
12 muffins

300 g (10 oz) self-raising flour
3 teaspoons baking powder
75 g (3 oz) Parmesan cheese, grated
1 courgette, about 200 g (7 oz), coarsely grated
150 ml (5 fl oz) natural yogurt
3 tablespoons olive oil
3 eggs
3 tablespoons milk
salt and pepper

Put the flour, baking powder and cheese in a large mixing bowl. Add salt and pepper to taste.

Add the courgette to the bowl with the yogurt, oil, eggs and milk. Beat lightly together until just mixed.

Line a 12-section muffin tin with paper muffin cases and spoon the muffin mixture into the cases, filling each one two-thirds full. Bake in a preheated oven, 200°C (400°F), Gas Mark 6, for 18–20 minutes or until well risen and golden-brown. Serve warm or cold with bowls of hot soup or a little butter for a snack.

COOK'S NOTES These muffins freeze well in a plastic bag. Microwave from frozen one at a time or defrost at room temperature and add to lunch boxes. For a change try mixing a little grated carrot in place of some of the courgette.

Preparation time:
15 minutes

Serves: **6**

250 g (8 oz) Greek yogurt
5 tablespoons mayonnaise
3 spring onions, trimmed and finely chopped
100 g (3½ oz) feta cheese
salt and pepper

TO SERVE:
selection of vegetables, such as red and yellow pepper strips, radishes, cauliflower or broccoli florets, sugarsnap peas, carrot, cucumber and celery sticks

In a bowl mix together the yogurt and mayonnaise. Add the spring onions. Crumble the feta into the bowl and stir in gently. Season with pepper and a little salt if required.

Serve with an assortment of crunchy vegetable dippers. Alternatively, transfer to a container and seal tightly. It can be stored for up to 2 days in the refrigerator.

COOK'S NOTES The fresh, tangy flavour of feta cheese is perfect for dips, and the cheese is easy to blend with yogurt. Serve this dip with crisp vegetables sticks and grainy bread as an appetizing light lunch or picnic food. Leftover dip can be spooned over baked potatoes.

57 Couscous and bean salad

Preparation time:
10 minutes, plus standing and chilling

Cooking time:
2 minutes

Serves: **6–8**

250 g (8 oz) couscous
300 ml (½ pint) boiling water
100 g (3½ oz) French beans, trimmed
4 eggs, hard-boiled and shelled
150 g (5 oz) cherry tomatoes, halved
400 g (13 oz) can red kidney beans, rinsed and drained
small handful of flat leaf parsley, chopped
4 tablespoons olive oil
2 tablespoons lemon juice
2 teaspoons hot chilli sauce (optional)
salt and pepper

Put the couscous in a large bowl, pour on the boiling water, cover and leave to stand for 10 minutes or until the water has been absorbed.

Meanwhile, cut the French beans into bite-sized pieces and cook them in boiling salted water for about 2 minutes, drain and refresh under cold running water. Fluff up the couscous with a fork to separate any grains that are stuck together.

Roughly chop the hard-boiled eggs. Add the tomatoes, French beans, eggs, kidney beans and chopped parsley to the couscous.

Beat together the oil, lemon juice, chilli sauce (if used) and a little salt and pepper. Add this dressing to the salad and toss the ingredients together lightly. Chill until ready to serve.

58 Crunchy croûton salad

Preparation time:
20 minutes, plus chilling

Cooking time:
18 minutes

Oven temperature:
200°C (400°F), Gas Mark 6

Serves: **2**

4 thin-cut rashers of streaky bacon
2 slices of seeded or white bread
1 large avocado, stoned and peeled
1 small cos lettuce
25 g (1 oz) Parmesan cheese, grated
4 eggs, hard-boiled, shelled and cut in quarters

DRESSING:
3 tablespoons olive oil
1 tablespoon lemon juice or white wine vinegar
1 teaspoon grainy mustard

Cut the rind off the bacon. Put the bread in a shallow, ovenproof dish or roasting tin and lay the bacon on top. Bake in a preheated oven, 200°C (400°F), Gas Mark 6, for 10 minutes.

Meanwhile, chop the avocado flesh into small chunks. Tear the lettuce into bite-sized pieces and mix them in a bowl.

Move the bacon to one side of the baking dish or tin and scatter cheese over the bread. Return the dish to the oven and bake for a further 8 minutes or until the cheese has melted over the bread and is beginning to colour. Transfer the bacon and cheese toasts to a plate to cool.

Make the dressing by mixing together the oil, lemon juice or vinegar and the mustard in a small bowl.

Break the cool bacon and cheese toast into small pieces and scatter them over the lettuce with the avocado and egg quarters. Pour over the dressing and lightly mix it in. Chill until needed.

COOK'S NOTES Bulgar wheat is a great and healthy alternative to couscous. Soak in boiling water and use in the same way.

59 Minted pasta salad

60 Jewelled couscous

Preparation time:
15 minutes

Cooking time:
3–4 minutes

Serves: 6–8

200 g (7 oz) soup pasta or small pasta
    shapes
1/2 charentais or ogen melon
100 g (31/2 oz) sliced ham, roughly diced
250 g (8 oz) courgettes, coarsely grated
1 tablespoon clear honey
2 tablespoons lemon juice
3 tablespoons light olive oil
3 tablespoons chopped mint
salt and pepper

Preparation time:
15 minutes, plus standing
and chilling

Cooking time:
2 minutes

Serves: 2–3

150 g (5 oz) couscous
200 ml (7 fl oz) hot vegetable stock
50 g (2 oz) green beans, trimmed
1/2 small pineapple
1 pomegranate
finely grated rind of 1/2 orange and
    3 tablespoons juice
2 tablespoons olive oil
1 tablespoon clear honey
1 small red pepper, cored, deseeded
    and diced

Cook the pasta in plenty of boiling water for about 3–4 minutes or until just tender. Drain and rinse under cold running water.

Discard the seeds and skin from the melon and cut the flesh into small dice. Mix the pasta, melon, ham and courgettes in a bowl.

Beat the honey, lemon juice, oil, mint and a little salt and pepper in a small bowl. Pour the dressing over the salad and toss gently to mix. Chill until required.

Put the couscous in a heatproof bowl and add the stock. Leave to stand for 20 minutes.

Meanwhile, cook the beans in boiling water for 2 minutes. Drain, rinse in cold water and cut them into 1 cm (1/2 inch) lengths.

Cut the pineapple into chunky slices, discard the core and skin and chop the flesh into small pieces. Cut the pomegranate in half. Pull the fruit apart and ease out the clusters of seeds. Separate the seeds, discarding any white parts of the fruit.

Mix the orange rind and juice with the oil and honey.

Add the beans, chopped fruit and red pepper to the couscous and pour over the dressing. Mix well and chill until needed.

COOK'S NOTES Pasta salads are great for lunchboxes and provide a welcome change from the usual sandwiches and rolls. This salad can be made in advance and kept in the refrigerator for up to 2 days. Use halved seedless grapes, diced pear, apple slices or orange segments instead of melon if you prefer.

61 Lunchbox jambalaya　62 Mini pasta salad

Preparation time:
20 minutes, plus chilling

Cooking time:
25 minutes

Serves: 2

100 g (3¹/₂ oz) long-grain rice
2 tablespoons olive oil
1 boneless, skinless chicken breast fillet,
　diced
1 celery stick, thinly sliced
1 green pepper, cored, deseeded and
　diced
15 g (¹/₂ oz) fresh root ginger, peeled and
　grated
1 teaspoon ground paprika
¹/₂ teaspoon ground turmeric
¹/₂ teaspoon dried mixed herbs
150 ml (¹/₄ pint) chicken or vegetable
　stock
6 cherry tomatoes, halved

Cook the rice, uncovered, in plenty of boiling water in a medium-sized saucepan for about 12 minutes or until it is tender. Drain thoroughly.

Heat 1 tablespoon oil in a large, nonstick frying pan, add the chicken and fry it gently, stirring, for 5 minutes. Add the celery and green pepper and fry for a further 3 minutes. Add the ginger, paprika, turmeric, herbs and stock to the pan and cook gently for 5 minutes or until the stock has almost evaporated.

Stir the cherry tomatoes into the frying pan together with the rice and remaining oil. Mix all the ingredients together well and transfer to a bowl to cool. Chill overnight.

COOK'S NOTES Make this savoury rice dish the day before so it has plenty of time to chill thoroughly overnight. Instead of chicken you could use prawns, chopped pork or chorizo sausage.

Preparation time:
15 minutes, plus chilling

Cooking time:
3–4 minutes

Serves: 2

50 g (2 oz) small pasta shapes
2 tablespoons sunflower oil
1 teaspoon sun-dried or ordinary tomato
　paste
1 teaspoon wine vinegar
¹/₂ small carrot, diced
¹/₄ red pepper, deseeded and diced
1 tomato, diced
50 g (2 oz) medium Cheddar cheese,
　diced

Cook the pasta in a large saucepan of boiling water until it is just tender to the bite.

Meanwhile, mix the oil, tomato paste and vinegar in a bowl until evenly blended. Add the carrot, red pepper, tomato and cheese and toss to mix well.

Drain the pasta, rinse under cold running water and drain thoroughly. Add the pasta to the salad, toss together and chill overnight.

63 Mini vegetable frittatas   64 Baby tortillas

Preparation time:
15 minutes

Cooking time:
14–15 minutes

Oven temperature:
190°C (375°F), Gas Mark 5

Makes:
12 frittatas

250 g (8 oz) baking potatoes, peeled and cubed
125 g (4 oz) frozen mixed vegetables
75 g (3 oz) Cheddar, Gruyère or Emmental cheese, grated
oil, for greasing
6 eggs
150 ml (¹/₄ pint) milk
salt and pepper

TO SERVE:
vegetable sticks
tomato ketchup

Put the potatoes in a large saucepan with the frozen vegetables, cover with cold water and bring to the boil. Cook for 4 minutes or until the potatoes are just tender. Drain.

Spoon the cheese and the vegetables into a lightly oiled 12-section muffin tin.

In a large jug beat together the eggs and milk. Season with salt and pepper and pour the mixture equally over the potatoes and vegetables. Cook in a preheated oven, 190°C (375°F), Gas Mark 5, for 10 minutes or until the tops are golden and the eggs are set. Serve warm or cold with vegetable sticks and ketchup.

Preparation time:
15 minutes

Cooking time:
25 minutes

Oven temperature:
180°C (350°F), Gas Mark 4

Makes:
12 tortillas

375 g (12 oz) baby potatoes, thinly sliced
oil, for greasing
1 small onion, finely chopped
6 eggs
25 g (1 oz) Parmesan cheese, grated
salt and pepper

Cook the potatoes in a lightly salted boiling water for 3–4 minutes or until just tender. Drain and transfer to a lightly oiled 12-section muffin tin. Scatter over the chopped onion.

In a jug beat the eggs with the cheese. Season with a little salt and pepper and pour the mixture equally over the potatoes. Bake in a preheated oven, 180°C (350°F), Gas Mark 4, for about 20 minutes or until the eggs have just set. Loosen the edges of the tortillas with a palette knife and transfer to a plate. Leave to cool.

COOK'S NOTES These small tortillas are perfect for lunchboxes because they have a more intense flavour when eaten cold. Try sprinkling additional flavourings, such as chopped sun-dried tomatoes, pine nuts or shredded Parma ham, over the potatoes before adding the eggs.

65 Breadsticks

66 Sausage pizza squares

Preparation time:
20 minutes, plus proving

Cooking time:
6–8 minutes

Oven temperature:
200°C (400°F), Gas Mark 6

Makes:
25 sticks

500 g (1 lb) strong plain bread flour, plus extra for kneading
1 teaspoon salt
1 teaspoon fast-action dried yeast
1 teaspoon caster sugar
1 tablespoon fennel seeds
4 tablespoons sesame seeds
300 ml (1/2 pint) lukewarm milk
oil, for greasing

Put the flour, salt, yeast and sugar in a mixing bowl. Roughly crush the fennel seeds in a pestle and mortar and add them to the flour mixture with the sesame seeds.

Gradually mix the milk into the flour mixture with a wooden spoon, then use your hands to bring the mixture together to a soft but not sticky dough. Add a little warm water if necessary.

Turn out the dough on a lightly floured surface and knead for 5 minutes or until it is smooth and elastic. Return the dough to the bowl, cover with clingfilm and leave to rise in a warm place for 45–60 minutes or until it has doubled in size.

Knock back the dough (knead it for a further 5 minutes or until it is smooth and elastic) and cut it into 25 pieces. Roll each out to make a rope 25 cm (10 inches) long.

Space the breadsticks slightly apart on lightly oiled baking sheets. Cover with lightly oiled clingfilm and leave to rise in a warm place for 20–30 minutes or until they are half as big again.

Bake the breadsticks in a preheated oven, 200°C (400°F), Gas Mark 6, for 6–8 minutes or until they are pale golden. Serve cold.

Preparation time:
20 minutes, plus proving

Cooking time:
10–12 minutes

Oven temperature:
220°C (425°F), Gas Mark 7

Makes:
6 pizzas

400 g (13 oz) strong white flour, plus extra for dusting
1/4 teaspoon salt
1 teaspoon caster sugar
1 1/2 teaspoons fast-action dried yeast
2 tablespoons olive oil, plus extra for greasing
200–250 ml (7–8 fl oz) lukewarm water

TOPPING:
4 tablespoons tomato sauce (ketchup)
3 tomatoes, diced
small bunch of basil
4 cooked sausages, thinly sliced
4 chilled frankfurters, thickly sliced
75 g (3 oz) Cheddar cheese, grated

Put the flour, salt, sugar and yeast in a large mixing bowl. Add the oil and gradually mix in just enough of the water to make a soft but not sticky dough. Use a wooden spoon at first, then bring the dough together with your hands.

Turn out the dough on a lightly floured surface and knead it for 5 minutes or until it is smooth and elastic. Roll out the dough very thinly to a rectangle, about 37.5 x 25 cm (15 x 10 inches), then cut it into 6 equal squares. Arrange the squares on lightly oiled baking sheets so that there is space for the dough to rise and spread.

Spread the top of the pizzas with tomato sauce, leaving a border of dough still showing. Arrange the tomatoes on top. Tear the basil into pieces and sprinkle on the top. Arrange the sausage and frankfurter slices on top of the tomatoes and sprinkle over the cheese. Leave the pizzas (uncovered) in a warm place for 30 minutes to rise.

Bake the pizzas in a preheated oven, 220°C (425°F), Gas Mark 7, for 10–12 minutes or until the cheese is bubbling. Serve warm.

67 Basil, garlic and cheese twist

68 Soft seeded granary rolls

Preparation time:
20 minutes, plus proving

Cooking time:
15 minutes

Oven temperature:
200°C (400°F), Gas Mark 6

Makes:
2 loaves

400 g (13 oz) strong white flour, plus extra
  for dusting
¹/₄ teaspoon salt
1 teaspoon caster sugar
1¹/₂ teaspoons fast-action dried yeast
2 tablespoons sunflower oil, plus extra
  for greasing
200–250 ml (7–8 fl oz) lukewarm water
50 g (2 oz) butter, softened
3 garlic cloves, crushed
small bunch of basil
125 g (4 oz) Cheddar cheese, grated

Preparation time:
20 minutes, plus proving

Cooking time:
8–10 minutes

Oven temperature:
200°C (400°F), Gas Mark 6

Makes:
16 rolls

400 g (13 oz) granary flour, plus extra for
  dusting
¹/₄ teaspoon salt
1¹/₂ teaspoons fast-action dried yeast
3 teaspoons clear honey
1 tablespoon olive or sunflower oil, plus
  extra for greasing
200–250 ml (7–8 fl oz) lukewarm water
1 egg yolk, beaten
sunflower, poppy and sesame seeds

Put the flour, salt, sugar and yeast in a mixing bowl. Add the oil and mix in just enough warm water to make a soft but not sticky dough. Use a wooden spoon at first, then bring the dough together with your hands.

Turn out the dough on a lightly floured surface and knead for 5 minutes or until it is smooth and elastic.

Roll out the dough thinly to make a rectangle about 25 x 45 cm (10 x 18 inches). Spread the dough with the butter and add the garlic evenly. Tear the basil leaves from the stems, reserving a few for the top of the dough, and sprinkle over the butter and garlic. Reserving some for the top, sprinkle cheese over the dough.

Roll up the dough, starting at one of the longer edges. Twist the roll several times and cut it in half to make 2 loaves.

Put the loaves on a lightly oiled baking sheet, leaving a space between them, and sprinkle with the reserved basil leaves and cheese. Cover loosely with lightly oiled clingfilm and leave in a warm place for 30 minutes to rise. Bake in a preheated oven, 200°C (400°F), Gas Mark 6, for 15 minutes or until the loaves are golden-brown and the bases sound hollow when tapped with your fingertips.

Put the flour, salt and yeast in the bowl. Add the honey and oil and gradually mix in just enough of the water to mix to a soft but not sticky dough. Use a wooden spoon at first, then bring the dough together with your hands.

Knead the dough on a lightly floured surface for 5 minutes or until it is smooth and elastic. Cut the dough into quarters, then cut each quarter into 4 more pieces. Shape each piece into a ball and arrange them in rows of 4 on a lightly oiled baking sheet, leaving space between each ball for the rolls to rise and spread. Cover loosely with lightly oiled clingfilm and leave to rise in a warm place for 30–40 minutes or until the rolls are half as big again.

Brush the rolls with egg yolk and sprinkle each row of rolls with a different kind of seed. Bake in a preheated oven, 200°C (400°F), Gas Mark 6, for 8–10 minutes or until the rolls are well risen and browned and the bases sound hollow when tapped with your fingertips. Leave the rolls to cool on the baking sheet and serve warm or cold with butter.

4 Meat, fish and poultry

69 Bolognese

Preparation time:
15 minutes

Cooking time:
1¼ hours

Serves: **4–5**

25 g (1 oz) butter
2 tablespoons olive oil
1 onion, finely chopped
2 celery sticks, finely chopped
2 garlic cloves, crushed
500 g (1 lb) lean minced beef
200 g (7 oz) spicy Italian sausages, skinned
300 ml (½ pint) beef stock
400 g (13 oz) can chopped tomatoes
1 teaspoon caster sugar
2 bay leaves
1 teaspoon dried oregano
2 tablespoons sun-dried tomato paste
salt and pepper

TO SERVE:
pasta, such as tagliatelle, linguini or spaghetti
grated Parmesan cheese

Melt the butter and oil in a large, heavy-based saucepan and gently fry the onion and celery for 5 minutes. Add the garlic, beef and skinned sausages and cook until they are lightly coloured, breaking up the beef and the sausages with a wooden spoon.

Add the stock and let the mixture bubble for 1–2 minutes or until it has slightly evaporated. Add the tomatoes, sugar, bay leaves, oregano, tomato paste and a little salt and pepper and bring just to the boil. Reduce the heat to its lowest setting, cover the pan with a lid and cook for about 1 hour, stirring occasionally, until thick and pulpy.

Serve the sauce with your child's favourite pasta and sprinkled with grated Parmesan.

70 Spicy meat and bean pasta

Preparation time:
20 minutes

Cooking time:
1¼ hours

Serves: **4–6**

1 tablespoon olive oil
1 medium onion, finely chopped
2 carrots, diced
2 garlic cloves, crushed
500 g (1 lb) lean minced lamb
1 teaspoon ground cinnamon
½ teaspoon ground allspice or nutmeg
400 g (13 oz) can chopped tomatoes
300 ml (½ pint) lamb or beef stock
250 g (8 oz) campania, fusilli or rigatoni pasta
100 g (3½ oz) green beans
100 g (3½ oz) frozen broad beans
3 tablespoons chopped mixed mint and parsley
salt and pepper

Heat the oil in a large, heavy-based saucepan, add the onion, carrot, garlic and minced lamb and fry for 5 minutes, stirring until the mince is evenly browned. Add the spices, tomatoes and stock and season to taste. Bring to the boil, breaking up the mince with a wooden spoon.

Cover the pan and simmer the mixture for 1 hour, stirring from time to time. Top up with extra stock if needed.

When the mince is almost cooked, cook the pasta in boiling water for 10–12 minutes or according to the instructions on the packet.

Cut the green beans in half and cook them in boiling water with the broad beans for 5 minutes or until just tender.

Drain the pasta, tip it back into the dry pan and stir in the mince mixture. Add the herbs to the drained beans. Spoon the pasta and mince into bowls and top with the beans. Serve immediately.

71 Quick pasta carbonara   72 Hoisin glazed beef

Preparation time:
15 minutes

Cooking time:
12–15 minutes

Serves: **4–6**

400 g (13 oz) dried spaghetti or other long, thin pasta
2 tablespoons olive oil
1 onion, finely chopped
200 g (7 oz) pancetta or streaky bacon, diced
2 garlic cloves, finely chopped
3 eggs
4 tablespoons grated Parmesan cheese
3 tablespoons chopped flat leaf parsley
3 tablespoons single cream
salt and pepper
green salad, to serve (optional)

Preparation time:
15 minutes

Cooking time:
about 5 minutes

Serves: **2**

1 sheet egg noodles, about 90 g (3¹/₄ oz)
1 tablespoon sunflower oil
1 carrot, cut into strips
¹/₂ red pepper, deseeded and cut into strips
75 g (3 oz) button mushrooms, sliced
300 g (10 oz) rump steak, fat trimmed, thinly sliced
2 spring onions, trimmed and thickly sliced
2 tablespoons hoisin sauce
3 tablespoons water
2 heads of pak choi, about 100 g (3¹/₂ oz) in total

Cook the pasta in a large saucepan of boiling salted water for 8–10 minutes or according to the instructions on the packet.

Meanwhile, heat the oil in a large, nonstick frying pan, add the onion and fry until it is soft. Add the pancetta or bacon and garlic and cook gently for 4–5 minutes.

Beat the eggs with the Parmesan, parsley and cream. Season to taste and set aside.

Drain the pasta and add it to the onion and pancetta. Stir over a gentle heat until combined, then pour in the egg mixture. Stir and remove the pan from the heat. Continue mixing well for a few seconds, until the eggs are lightly cooked and creamy, then serve immediately with a green salad, if liked.

Soak the noodles in boiling water or cook in a saucepan of boiling water according to the packet instructions. Drain and keep warm.

Meanwhile, heat the oil in a wok or heavy-based, nonstick frying pan, add the carrot, red pepper and mushrooms and stir-fry for 2 minutes. Add the steak and spring onions and stir-fry for 2–3 minutes, until the steak has browned.

Add the hoisin sauce and the water, then add the pak choi and cook for 1 minute, until the green leaves have just wilted.

Spoon the drained noodles into bowls, top with the stir-fry and serve.

COOK'S NOTES This colourful stir-fry is a good way to get a small amount of meat to go a long way.

73 Juicy burgers

74 Pork stir-fry

Preparation time:
15 minutes

Cooking time:
about 16 minutes

Serves: **4**

**500 g (1 lb) lean or low-fat minced lamb
or beef
2 carrots, grated
3 teaspoons tomato purée
2 tablespoons chopped parsley
salt and pepper
vegetable oil, for frying
4 burger buns**

TO GARNISH:
**crispy lettuce
tomatoes, sliced
onions, cut into rings**

Preparation time:
15 minutes

Cooking time:
15 minutes

Serves: **4**

**2 tablespoons vegetable oil
2 garlic cloves, finely chopped
1 teaspoon grated fresh root ginger
1 chilli, deseeded and diced
1 red pepper, cored, deseeded and cut
into strips
3 carrots, cut into strips
1 large onion, sliced
250 g (8 oz) lean pork, cubed
1 courgette, sliced
1 small broccoli head, divided into florets
Thai rice, to serve**

SAUCE:
**2 tablespoons soy sauce
2 tablespoons orange juice
1 teaspoon tomato purée
1 teaspoon vinegar
1 teaspoon demerara sugar**

Mix the meat, carrot, tomato purée and parsley in a bowl. Add salt and pepper to taste. Shape the mixture into 4 burgers.

Lightly oil a frying pan and cook the burgers for about 8 minutes on each side. Alternatively, grill under a medium-high heat for the same length of time.

Cut each burger bun in half horizontally. Place a layer of lettuce on the base of the bottom bun and put the burger on top. Add the tomatoes and onion and cover with the top of the bun.

Heat the oil in a wok or large, nonstick frying pan and add the garlic, ginger and chilli to heat through. Do not allow them to colour.

Add the pepper, carrots, onion and pork and stir-fry over a moderate to high heat for about 5 minutes. Add the courgette and broccoli and continue to stir-fry for a further 5 minutes.

Stir in the sauce ingredients and allow to bubble in the base of the wok, then toss the ingredients through the liquid as you stir-fry for a few more minutes.

Serve with steamed or boiled fragrant Thai rice.

COOK'S NOTES Homemade burgers made with lean red meat need not be fatty, especially if they are grilled and served with a mixed salad and healthy homemade chips.

75 Ratatouille lamb pie

Preparation time:
20 minutes

Cooking time:
50 minutes

Oven temperature:
200°C (400°F), Gas Mark 6

Serves: **4–6**

500 g (1 lb) lean lamb fillet
3 tablespoons olive oil
1 small aubergine, about 300 g (10 oz), diced
2 onions, chopped
2 garlic cloves, crushed
400 g (13 oz) can chopped tomatoes
2 tablespoons sun-dried tomato paste
2 red peppers, cored, deseeded and roughly chopped
2 courgettes, sliced
1 tablespoon chopped thyme
3 sheets filo pastry, about 150 g (5 oz) in total
2 teaspoons sesame seeds
salt and pepper
thyme sprigs, to garnish

Trim any fat from the lamb and cut the meat into pieces. Process briefly in a food processor until chopped into small pieces.

Heat 2 tablespoons oil in a large, nonstick frying pan or heavy-based pan. Add the lamb, aubergine and onions and fry for 5–10 minutes or until browned. Add the garlic, tomatoes, tomato paste, red peppers, courgettes, thyme and a little salt and pepper and bring to the boil. Reduce the heat, cover and cook for 20 minutes or until the lamb is tender and the sauce is pulpy. Turn into a shallow, 1.8 litre (3 pint) pie dish.

On a clean surface crumple up 1 filo sheet roughly to the dimensions of the pie dish and brush with a little oil. Crumple another sheet over this one and brush with more oil. Crumple the final filo sheet on top. Carefully lift the pastry over the filling, easing it to fit so the edges just cover the rim of the pie dish.

Brush with the remaining oil and scatter with the sesame seeds. Bake in a preheated oven, 200°C (400°F), Gas Mark 6, for about 20 minutes or until the pastry is golden. Serve garnished with thyme.

76 Indonesian beef noodles

Preparation time:
15 minutes

Cooking time:
10 minutes

Serves: **4–6**

250 g (8 oz) fine rice noodles or ribbon noodles
375 g (12 oz) lean steak
2 tablespoons sunflower or vegetable oil
3 garlic cloves, sliced
1 bunch of spring onions, trimmed and roughly chopped
5 cm (2 inches) fresh root ginger, grated
4 tablespoons peanut butter
1 tablespoon dark soy sauce
finely grated rind and juice of 1 lime
1 teaspoon light muscovado sugar
900 ml (1½ pints) chicken stock
50 g (2 oz) roasted cashew nuts
100 g (3½ oz) mangetout, halved

Soak the noodles in boiling water or cook in a saucepan of boiling water according to the packet instructions. Drain and keep warm.

Meanwhile, trim any fat from the beef and cut the meat into thin strips. Heat the oil in a wok or large, nonstick frying pan, add the beef and fry quickly for 2 minutes. Remove with a slotted spoon and set aside.

Add the garlic, spring onions and ginger to the pan and fry for 1 minute. Add the peanut butter, soy sauce, lime rind and juice, sugar and stock and bring to the boil. Reduce the heat, cover the pan and cook gently for 5 minutes.

Return the beef to the pan and add the noodles, cashew nuts and mangetout. Cook gently for 2 minutes. Serve immediately in warm bowls or shallow serving dishes.

COOK'S NOTES You could use boneless chicken breast or pork fillet instead of beef if you prefer. Rice noodles are made from rice flour and water and are available dried from larger supermarkets. If you wish use fine egg noodles instead.

77 Sticky barbecued ribs   78 Mediterranean stew

Preparation time:
15 minutes

Cooking time:
1¼ hours

Oven temperature:
200°C (400°F), Gas Mark 6

Serves: **4–6**

1.25 kg (2½ lb) pork ribs, rinsed and drained
5 tablespoons tomato ketchup
3 tablespoons soft light brown sugar
2 tablespoons sunflower oil
2 tablespoons Worcestershire sauce
2 teaspoons Dijon mustard
450 ml (¾ pint) chicken stock
2 oranges, cut in wedges, to garnish
salad, to serve

Put the ribs in a roasting tin.

In a small bowl mix together the ketchup, sugar, oil, Worcestershire sauce and mustard. Brush the mixture over the ribs. Pour the stock into the base of the tin.

Roast in a preheated oven, 200°C (400°F), Gas Mark 6, for 1¼ hours, brushing once or twice with pan juices and turning over any very brown ribs. Transfer the ribs to serving plates, decorate with orange wedges and serve with salad.

COOK'S NOTES Most children love food they can eat with their hands so these tasty ribs are sure to be a winner with your little ones.

Preparation time:
15 minutes

Cooking time:
45 minutes

Serves: **4–6**

2 tablespoons olive oil
250 g (8 oz) lean lamb fillet, thinly sliced
1 red onion, chopped
1 large aubergine, about 375 g (12 oz), diced
2 garlic cloves, crushed
400 g (13 oz) can chopped tomatoes
2 tablespoons sun-dried tomato paste
1 teaspoon light muscovado sugar
150 ml (¼ pint) vegetable stock
300 g (10 oz) can red kidney beans, rinsed and drained
salt and pepper
snipped chives, to garnish
crusty bread, to serve

PESTO:
½ bunch of spring onions, trimmed and roughly chopped
50 g (2 oz) Parmesan cheese, crumbled
2 teaspoons wine vinegar or lemon juice
3 tablespoons olive oil

Heat 1 tablespoon oil in a heavy-based saucepan, add the lamb and fry gently for 5 minutes.

In a separate pan heat a further 1 tablespoon oil, add the onion and aubergine and fry for about 5 minutes. Add the garlic, tomatoes, tomato paste, sugar and stock and bring to the boil. Reduce the heat, cover and simmer for 5 minutes. Ladle about three-quarters of the mixture over the lamb and cook gently for 15 minutes. Add the red kidney beans to the remaining mixture and cook for 15 minutes. Check the seasoning.

Make the pesto. Put all the ingredients in a food processor and process to a coarse paste. Transfer to a small bowl. Ladle the stew into warm bowls. Garnish with chives and serve with the pesto and crusty bread.

79 Beef with colcannon

Preparation time:
25 minutes

Cooking time:
about 1¼ hours

Serves: **6**

1 kg (2 lb) lean casserole steak
2 tablespoons plain flour
2 tablespoons sunflower or vegetable oil
2 onions, chopped
900 ml (1½ pints) beef stock
3 bay leaves
4 pickled walnuts, quartered
salt and pepper

COLCANNON:
1 kg (2 lb) potatoes, cut into chunks
500 g (1 lb) Savoy cabbage or spring greens, roughly shredded
25 g (1 oz) butter
1 onion, chopped
4 tablespoons semi-skimmed milk

Cut the beef into small chunks, discarding any excess fat. Season the flour and use it to coat the meat. Heat the oil in a large, heavy-based saucepan, add half the beef and fry quickly until browned. Remove with a slotted spoon and fry the remainder.

Return all the beef to the pan with the onions and fry for 2 minutes. Add the stock and bay leaves. Bring just to the boil, lower the heat, cover the pan and simmer gently for 1 hour or until the beef is tender. Stir in the pickled walnuts.

Meanwhile, make the colcannon. Cook the potatoes in lightly salted boiling water for about 20 minutes or until tender. Add the cabbage to the pan and cook for a further 5 minutes. Melt the butter in a nonstick frying pan, add the onion and fry for 5 minutes.

Drain the potato and cabbage and return to the saucepan. Add the onion and milk and mash well. Serve the colcannon immediately with the piping hot beef stew.

80 Lamb balti

Preparation time:
20 minutes

Cooking time:
about 55 minutes

Serves: **6**

625 g (1¼ lb) lean lamb fillet or leg
1 tablespoon minced ginger
2 garlic cloves, crushed
150 ml (¼ pint) natural yogurt
12 cardamom pods
2 tablespoons sunflower or vegetable oil
2 large onions, cut into wedges
1 cinnamon stick, halved
1 teaspoon ground turmeric
1 teaspoon cumin seeds
2 bay leaves
2 teaspoons medium curry paste
250 g (8 oz) can chopped tomatoes
450 ml (¾ pint) lamb or chicken stock
625 g (1¼ lb) potatoes, cut into small chunks
3 tablespoons chopped fresh coriander
salt and pepper
naan bread or rice, to serve

Cut the lamb into small chunks and discard any fat. Put the lamb, ginger, garlic and yogurt in a heavy-based frying pan and heat until bubbling. Reduce the heat, cover the pan and simmer for 20 minutes.

Meanwhile, pound the cardamom pods to expose the seeds. Heat the oil in a saucepan, add the cardamoms, onions, cinnamon, turmeric, cumin and bay leaves, season to taste and fry gently for 5 minutes.

Add the lamb mixture, curry paste, tomatoes and stock and bring to a simmer. Cover and cook for 15 minutes or until the lamb is tender and the sauce has thickened slightly.

Add the potatoes and cook, covered, for a further 15 minutes or until they are tender. Stir in the coriander and serve immediately with naan bread or rice to mop up the juices.

81 Toad in the hole

82 Couscous with grilled sausages

Preparation time:
15 minutes

Cooking time:
25 minutes

Oven temperature:
220°C (425°F), Gas Mark 7

Serves: **4**

125 g (4 oz) plain flour
2 tablespoons thyme leaves
1 egg
300 ml (½ pint) semi-skimmed milk or
  milk and water mixed
8 rashers of streaky bacon
500 g (1 lb) lean pork sausages
2 tablespoons sunflower oil
salt and pepper

Preparation time:
15 minutes, plus soaking

Cooking time:
10 minutes

Serves: **4**

500 g (1 lb) lean pork sausages
125 g (4 oz) couscous
25 g (1 oz) sultanas
200 ml (7 fl oz) boiling water
50 g (2 oz) green beans, thickly sliced
50 g (2 oz) frozen peas
2 tomatoes, chopped
2 tablespoons orange juice
1 garlic clove, crushed
2 tablespoons olive oil
salt and pepper

Put the flour and salt and pepper into the bowl. Add the thyme and egg. Gradually whisk in the milk or milk and water until the batter is smooth and frothy.

Stretch each rasher of bacon by running the flat of a knife along the rasher until it is half as long again. Wrap each bacon rasher around each of the sausages.

Pour the oil into a roasting tin and add the bacon-wrapped sausages. Cook in a preheated oven, 220°C (425°F), Gas Mark 7, for 5 minutes or until sizzling.

Whisk the batter again and quickly pour it over the sausage. Return the tin to the oven and cook for about 20 minutes or until the batter is well risen and golden. Serve hot with baked beans.

Cook the sausages under a preheated grill for 10 minutes, turning once or twice so they are evenly cooked.

Meanwhile, put the couscous and sultanas in a bowl. Add the boiling water and leave to soak for 5 minutes.

Cook the beans and peas in boiling water for 4 minutes. Drain.

Stir the beans, peas, tomatoes, juice, garlic, oil and a little salt and pepper into the couscous and mix together well. Spoon on to plates and top with the sausages.

COOK'S NOTES Serve toad in the hole with baked beans or peas and gravy for a dinner-time feast.

83 French bean and chorizo omelette

84 Jumbo macaroni cheese

Preparation time:
5 minutes

Cooking time:
about 10 minutes

Serves: **2**

150 g (5 oz) frozen French beans
1 tablespoon olive oil
15 g (½ oz) butter
1 red onion, chopped
4 eggs, beaten
25 g (1 oz) chorizo sausage, thinly sliced
50 g (2 oz) Cheddar cheese, grated
salt and pepper

TO SERVE:
crusty bread
tomato and olive salad

Preparation time:
15 minutes

Cooking time:
30 minutes

Oven temperature:
200°C (400°F), Gas Mark 6

Serves: **4**

250 g (8 oz) pasta quills or rigatoni
50 g (2 oz) butter
50 g (2 oz) plain flour
600 ml (1 pint) milk
200 g (7 oz) Gruyère or Cheddar cheese,
grated
1 teaspoon Dijon mustard (optional)
200 g (7 oz) frozen spinach, just defrosted
3 rashers of rindless back bacon,
cut in strips
125 g (4 oz) cherry tomatoes, halved
salt and pepper
watercress or salad, to serve

Cook the French beans in lightly salted boiling water and cook for 2 minutes. Drain.

Heat the oil and butter in an ovenproof, nonstick frying pan, add the onion and fry gently for 3 minutes or until softened. Add the eggs and season with salt and pepper. Cook gently for 2–3 minutes or until they are lightly set, pushing the cooked edges towards the centre so the uncooked mixture fills the pan.

Scatter the beans and chorizo over the surface of the omelette and then sprinkle over the cheese. Place under a preheated moderate grill for about 2 minutes or until the cheese has melted. Serve with warm, crusty bread and a simple tomato and olive salad

Cook the pasta in boiling water for 10 minutes or according to the instructions on the packet. Drain.

Meanwhile, gently heat the butter in another saucepan. Whisk in the flour, then gradually mix in the milk. Bring the sauce to the boil, whisking continually, until smooth and thick. Take the pan off the heat.

Keep about 4 tablespoons cheese for the top and whisk the rest into the sauce with the mustard (if used) and a little salt and pepper. Return to the heat and stir until the cheese melts. Stir in the pasta.

Squeeze any liquid from the spinach and spoon it into the base of an ovenproof dish. Add the pasta and sauce. Sprinkle the remaining cheese and then the bacon over the pasta. Arrange the tomatoes around the edge of the dish. Cook in a preheated oven, 200°C (400°F), Gas Mark 6, for 20 minutes or until the top is golden and the spinach is hot. Serve with sprigs of watercress or salad.

COOK'S NOTES Spicy, garlicky chorizo sausage is a great way of enlivening all kinds of dishes, from soups and stews to pilafs and pasta.

85 Turkey and cranberry pot pies

Preparation time:
40 minutes

Cooking time:
50–55 minutes

Oven temperature:
230°C (450°F), Gas Mark 8

Makes:
6 pies

**2 tablespoons vegetable oil
1 large onion, chopped
1 celery stick, chopped
2 tablespoons plain flour
475 ml (16 fl oz) chicken stock
300 ml (1/2 pint) double cream
500 g (1 lb) sweet potatoes, peeled and
   roughly chopped
8 small shallots
250 g (8 oz) button mushrooms, halved or
   sliced
375 g (12 oz) smoked turkey, roughly
   chopped
25 g (1 oz) dried cranberries, chopped
2 tablespoons chopped parsley
500 g (1 lb) puff pastry (thawed if frozen)
1 egg, beaten
salt and pepper
green beans, to serve**

Heat the oil in a nonstick frying pan and fry the onion and celery until golden-brown. Stir in the flour. Remove from the heat and add the stock, whisking to remove lumps. Return to the heat and whisk until smooth.

Add the cream and heat gently. Season to taste. Add the sweet potatoes, shallots, mushrooms, turkey, cranberries and parsley and stir to combine. Simmer gently for 10 minutes, leave to cool then divide the mixture among 6 small ovenproof dishes.

Roll out the pastry to 5 mm (1/4 inch) thick and cut circles 2.5 cm (1 inch) wider than the diameter of the dishes. Brush the rims with beaten egg and put a pastry circle on top of each dish, gently pressing the pastry to secure. Cut a small hole in each and decorate with any remaining pastry.

Bake in a preheated oven, 230°C (450°F), Gas Mark 8, for 30–35 minutes, or until puffed and golden-brown. Serve with green beans.

86 Easy chicken pasta

Preparation time:
15 minutes

Cooking time:
about 15 minutes

Serves: **4**

**250 g (8 oz) macaroni, fusilli or small
   pasta quills
125 g (4 oz) mixed frozen vegetables
325 g (11 oz) boneless, skinless chicken
   breasts
1 tablespoon olive oil
1 garlic clove, crushed (optional)
6 tablespoons mayonnaise
salt and pepper
some grated Parmesan or Cheddar
   cheese, to finish (optional)**

Cook the pasta in boiling water for 10 minutes or according to the instructions on the packet. Add the frozen vegetables to the pasta for the last 2 minutes of the cooking time. Drain.

Rinse the chicken with cold water, pat dry on kitchen paper and cut the meat into small squares.

Heat the oil in a nonstick frying pan and add the chicken and garlic (if used). Fry, stirring occasionally, for about 5 minutes or until browned and cooked through.

Tip the pasta and vegetables back into the dry pan and add the mayonnaise and chicken. Season to taste. Toss together, spoon into bowls and serve sprinkled with a little cheese, if liked.

COOK'S NOTES For a quick and easy pasta bake, try grilling the pasta in an oven proof dish until the cheese is golden and melted.

87 Chicken stir fry

88 Chicken dippers with salsa

Preparation time:
20 minutes

Cooking time:
10 minutes

Serves: **4**

2 tablespoons vegetable oil
2 shallots, finely chopped
2.5 cm (1 inch) fresh root ginger, peeled and cut into thin strips
2 garlic cloves, crushed
4 boneless, skinless chicken breasts, each about 75 g (3 oz), thinly sliced
2 tablespoons hoisin sauce
2 tablespoons oyster sauce
1 tablespoon light soy sauce
50 g (2 oz) dried cranberries
4 salad onions, diagonally sliced
50 g (2 oz) bean sprouts or sliced green or red pepper or carrot strips

TO GARNISH:
vegetable oil, for deep-frying
handful of basil leaves
1 large red chilli, deseeded and finely sliced

Heat the oil in a wok or large, nonstick frying pan and stir-fry the shallots, ginger and garlic for 30 seconds. Add the chicken and stir-fry for 2 minutes or until golden-brown.

Add the hoisin, oyster and soy sauces and the cranberries and stir-fry for a further 2 minutes. Check that the chicken is cooked all the way through, then add the onions and bean sprouts or other vegetables and toss together for 3–4 minutes.

In a small saucepan containing about 2 cm (1/2 inch) of oil, deep-fry the basil leaves and red chilli in 2 batches for 10–30 seconds until crisp. Serve the chicken stir-fry garnished with the basil and chilli.

Preparation time:
15 minutes

Cooking time:
5–6 minutes

Serves: **4**

2 eggs, beaten
2 tablespoons milk
100 g (3 1/2 oz) bread
4 tablespoons grated Parmesan cheese
4 boneless, skinless chicken breasts, about 625 g (1 1/4 lb) in total, cut into long, thin slices
25 g (1 oz) butter
2 tablespoons sunflower oil
salt and pepper

SALSA:
2 tomatoes
1/4 cucumber
75 g (3 oz) sweetcorn (thawed if frozen)
1 tablespoon chopped fresh coriander

In a shallow bowl mix together the eggs, milk and a little salt and pepper together in a shallow bowl.

Tear the bread into pieces, put it in a blender or food processor and blend until it resembles fine breadcrumbs. Transfer to a second shallow bowl and mix with the cheese.

Dip a chicken strip into the egg, then roll it in the breadcrumbs. Repeat until all the chicken strips are coated.

Make the salsa. Cut the tomatoes and cucumber into tiny pieces (about sweetcorn size). Mix together with the sweetcorn and coriander.

Heat the butter and oil in a nonstick frying pan and add the chicken, a few pieces at a time, until they are all added. Cook for 5–6 minutes, turning several times until evenly browned. (Cook in 2 batches if the pan is not very big.) Arrange on serving plates together with spoonfuls of the salsa.

89 Chicken fillets with sweet soy glaze

90 Easy roast chicken

Preparation time:
10 minutes, plus marinating

Cooking time:
30 minutes

Oven temperature:
180°C (350°F), Gas Mark 4,

Serves: **4**

4 boneless, skinless chicken breast fillets
4 tablespoons dark soy sauce
3 tablespoons light muscovado sugar
2 garlic cloves, crushed
2 tablespoons white wine vinegar
100 ml (3¹/₂ fl oz) orange juice
pepper

TO SERVE:
steamed vegetables
rice or noodles

Slice each chicken fillet in half horizontally and arrange the chicken in a large, shallow, ovenproof dish, into which the fillets fit snugly.

Mix together the soy sauce, sugar, garlic, vinegar, orange juice and pepper and pour the mixture over the chicken. Cover and chill the dish until you are ready to cook.

Bake the chicken in a preheated oven, 180°C (350°F), Gas Mark 4, for 30 minutes or until it is cooked through. Transfer to serving plates and spoon the cooking juices over the meat. Serve immediately with steamed broccoli and rice.

Preparation time:
20 minutes, plus marinating

Cooking time:
1 hour

Oven temperature:
200°C (400°F), Gas Mark 6

Serves: **2**

2 chicken breasts, on the bone, each about 300 g (10 oz)
4 bay leaves
1 orange
200 g (7 oz) shallots
200 g (7 oz) parsnips, cut into chunks
200 g (7 oz) carrots, cut into chunks
400 g (13 oz) small new potatoes
6 garlic cloves, unpeeled
3 tablespoons olive oil
3 teaspoons clear honey
salt and pepper
orange wedges, to serve
bay leaves, to garnish
gravy, to serve

Make 2 slits in each chicken breast and place a bay leaf in each cut. Cut 2 slices of orange, halve each slice and slide a piece under each bay leaf. Put the chicken in a large roasting tin and squeeze over the juice from the remaining orange.

Arrange the vegetables and garlic around the chicken, drizzle with oil and season with salt and pepper. Cover loosely in clingfilm and refrigerate overnight.

Bake the chicken in a preheated oven, 200°C (400°F), Gas Mark 6, for 50 minutes, basting the chicken and vegetables from time to time and turning them when necessary. Drizzle with honey and cook for a further 10 minutes or until the chicken juices run clear when a skewer is inserted into the thickest part and the vegetables are golden. Lift the chicken and vegetables out of the roasting tin with a draining spoon. Serve with gravy and orange wedges and garnish with bay leaves.

COOK'S NOTES This dish is also delicious served over noodles with stir-fried vegetables.

Preparation time:
30 minutes

Cooking time:
1 hour 20 minutes

Oven temperature:
190°C (375°F), Gas Mark 5

Serves: **4–5**

1.5 kg (3 lb) oven-ready chicken
2 teaspoons coriander seeds
1 teaspoon fennel seeds
1 teaspoon cumin seeds
2 tablespoons olive oil
1/2 teaspoon turmeric
1/2 teaspoon paprika
2 parsnips, cut into chunks
2 large carrots, cut into chunks
2 sweet potatoes, cut into chunks
1 large onion, cut into chunks
8 garlic cloves, unpeeled
2 tablespoons plain flour
600 ml (1 pint) chicken stock
fresh coriander leaves, to garnish

Remove any giblets and rinse the chicken inside and out with cold water. Drain and place in a large roasting tin.

Crush the seeds and put them in a plastic bag with the oil and ground spice. Shake until well mixed. Spoon a little of the mixture over the chicken breast, then cover it with foil. Roast the chicken in a preheated oven, 190°C (375°F), Gas Mark 5, for 1 hour 20 minutes.

Meanwhile, add the vegetables to the bag of spiced oil and toss. Add to the roasting tin after 20 minutes of cooking the chicken, tucking some garlic cloves between the chicken legs and adding the rest to the vegetables. Cook for 1 hour until golden, turning the vegetables after 30 minutes and removing the foil from the chicken at this point.

Transfer the chicken and vegetables to a large serving plate and keep warm. Garnish with coriander.

Drain the fat from the meat juices and stir in the flour. Make the gravy by putting the roasting tin on the hob and cooking for 1 minute, stirring. Gradually stir in the stock and bring to the boil. Strain into a jug and serve immediately.

Preparation time: **15 minutes, plus chilling**

Cooking time: **10 minutes**

Serves: **4**

1 tablespoon olive oil
1 large red onion, thinly sliced
1 red pepper, cored, deseeded and thinly sliced
1 yellow pepper, cored, deseeded and thinly sliced
450 g (14 1/2 oz) boneless, skinless chicken breasts, sliced into thin strips
1/8 teaspoon paprika
1/8 teaspoon mild chilli powder
1/8 teaspoon cumin
1/4 teaspoon oregano
4 soft flour tortillas
1/2 iceberg lettuce, finely shredded
Guacamole (see recipe 45), to serve (optional)

TOMATO SALSA:
1 small red onion, finely chopped
425 g (14 oz) small vine-ripened tomatoes
2 garlic cloves, crushed
large handful of fresh coriander leaves, chopped
pepper

Make the salsa. Combine the onion, tomatoes, garlic and coriander in a bowl. Season with pepper, cover and chill for 30 minutes.

Heat the oil in a wok or large, nonstick frying pan. Add the onion and peppers and stir-fry for 3–4 minutes. Add the chicken, spices and herbs, and cook for a further 5 minutes or until the chicken is cooked through.

Meanwhile, wrap the tortillas in foil and warm them in the oven for 5 minutes or according to the instructions on the packet. Spoon one-quarter of the chicken mixture into the centre of each tortilla, add a couple of tablespoons of salsa and some shredded lettuce. Roll up and serve warm, accompanied by guacamole, if liked.

93 Chicken with lemon and butternut squash

94 Wok around the clock stir-fry

Preparation time: **10 minutes**	**8 chicken thighs, skin on** **1 butternut squash, about 1 kg (2 lb),** **peeled, deseeded and cut into large**
Cooking time: **30–40 minutes**	**chunks** **2 red onions, cut into wedges** **8 garlic cloves**
Oven temperature: **200°C (400°F), Gas Mark 6**	**2 small lemons** **1 tablespoon clear honey** **2 tablespoons olive oil**
Serves: **4**	**6 rosemary sprigs** **pepper**

Arrange the chicken thighs, butternut squash, onion and 6 of the garlic cloves in a single layer in a large roasting tin (or use 2 medium tins). Grate the rind from 1 lemon and squeeze the juice and set aside. Slice the other lemon into wedges and add to the roasting tin.

Crush or finely chop the remaining garlic and mix with the lemon rind and juice, honey and oil. Pour the mixture over the chicken and vegetables. Sprinkle over the rosemary and season with pepper.

Bake in a preheated oven, 200°C (400°F), Gas Mark 6, for 30–40 minutes or until the chicken is cooked through.

Preparation time: **15 minutes**	**50 g (2 oz) mangetout** **50 g (2 oz) red pepper** **50 g (2 oz) carrot**
Cooking time: **10–11 minutes**	**2 spring onions, trimmed and cut into** **strips** **300 g (10 oz) boneless, skinless chicken**
Serves: **2**	**breast** **2 tablespoons corn or groundnut oil** **50 g (2 oz) baby corn or frozen sweetcorn** **50 g (2 oz) small broccoli florets** **2 garlic cloves, crushed** **1 teaspoon tamari sauce** **1 teaspoon sesame oil** **rice noodles, to serve (optional)**

Cut the mangetout, red pepper, carrot and spring onions into fine strips. Slice the chicken into strips 1 cm (1/2 inch) wide.

Heat the oil in a wok or large, nonstick frying pan. Add the chicken and cook, stirring, over a high heat for about 5 minutes or until it is golden-brown. Add the mangetout, pepper, carrots, spring onions, baby corn, broccoli and crushed garlic cloves and cook for 1–2 minutes. Turn the heat down to medium, cover with a lid and cook for a further 3–4 minutes.

Stir in the tamari sauce and sesame oil and serve immediately with rice noodles, if liked.

COOK'S NOTES Butternut squash is delicious and packed full of vitamins. However, if your children aren't keen try making this dish with sweet potato instead.

COOK'S NOTES This stir-fry can also be made using tofu or salmon fillet instead of the chicken. For a more substantial meal serve the stir-fry on a bed of rice

95 Peking duck

Preparation time:
20 minutes

Cooking time:
about 20 minutes

Oven temperature:
220°C (425°F), Gas Mark 7

Serves: **4**

1 tablespoon honey
1 tablespoon tamari sauce
4 boneless, skinless duck breasts
4 baby gem lettuces, finely shredded
1/2 cucumber, cut into strips
**4 spring onions, trimmed and cut into
  strips**
16 rice paper wrappers

SAUCE:
250 g (8 oz) pitted dates
250 ml (8 fl oz) water
3 teaspoons balsamic vinegar
3 teaspoons sesame oil

Combine the honey and tamari sauce and rub the mixture over the duck breasts. Put them on an oiled baking sheet, cover with foil and bake in a preheated oven, 220°C (425°F), Gas Mark 7, for 20 minutes or until cooked through. Remove the duck from the oven and leave to stand for 5 minutes.

Meanwhile, make the sauce. Put the dates and water in a small saucepan and simmer for about 10 minutes or until the dates are soft. Transfer the mixture to a food processor or blender with the balsamic vinegar and sesame oil and purée until smooth.

Brush both sides of the rice paper wrappers with water and allow them to stand for 2 minutes or until soft. Stack the wrappers in a bamboo steamer over a pan of boiling water. Cover the steamer and turn off the heat to keep the wrappers moist.

Slice the duck breasts and arrange the slices on a serving platter. Serve the steamed rice paper wrappers and vegetables on another platter and pour the sauce into a jug so your children can make their own rolls.

96 Chicken soup with barley

Preparation time:
20 minutes

Cooking time:
2¹/₂—3 hours

Serves: **8**

**1 large chicken, about 2.5 kg (5 lb), cut
  into quarters**
3 onions
3 large carrots
3 celery sticks
6 garlic cloves
4 bay leaves
50 g (2 oz) pearl barley
2 chicken stock cubes
4 tablespoons chopped parsley
salt and pepper (optional)

Put the chicken in a large saucepan with 1 quartered onion, 1 quartered carrot, 1 quartered celery stick, the garlic and bay leaves. Cover with water and bring to the boil. Cover the pan and simmer for 1–1¹/₂ hours, until the meat pulls away from the bones.

Remove the chicken pieces with a slotted spoon and allow to cool. Reserve the carrot, celery, onion and garlic.

Chop the chicken into bite-sized pieces and set aside. Keep the bones.

Skim any fat from the surface of the stock, return the chicken bones to the saucepan and add about 500 ml (1 pint) water. Bring to the boil, reduce the heat and simmer for 1 hour.

Strain the stock through a sieve and return the liquid to the saucepan. Put the reserved carrot, celery, onion and garlic cloves in a food processor or blender and add 1 ladleful of strained stock. Purée until smooth, then stir into the remaining stock.

Finely chop the remaining carrots, onions and celery and add them to the stock. Add the pearl barley and crumble in the stock cubes. Cook until the pearl barley and vegetables are tender. Add the chicken and parsley, season to taste, if liked, and serve.

97 Glazed chicken and peppers

98 Chicken with lemons and olives

Preparation time:
15 minutes

Cooking time:
40 minutes

Oven temperature:
220°C (425°F), Gas Mark 7

Serves: **4**

4 boneless, skinless chicken breasts
1 small onion, thinly sliced
2 red peppers, cored, deseeded and cut into chunks
2 orange or yellow peppers, cored, deseeded and cut into chunks
2 garlic cloves, crushed
3 tablespoons olive oil
2 courgettes, thickly sliced
salt and pepper

GLAZE:
1 tablespoon clear honey
2 teaspoons sweet chilli sauce
2 tablespoons tomato paste
1 tablespoon Worcestershire sauce
1 teaspoon cornflour
2 tablespoons orange juice

TO SERVE:
rice or baked potatoes
salad or green vegetables

Pat the chicken dry on kitchen paper and cut each breast into 6. Put the meat in a large roasting tin with the onion and peppers. Mix the garlic with the oil and salt and pepper, add to the roasting tin and toss the ingredients together. Bake in a preheated oven, 220°C (425°F), Gas Mark 7, for 15 minutes.

Add the courgettes to the tin and cook for a further 20 minutes or until the chicken is cooked and the vegetables are lightly coloured.

Meanwhile, make the glaze by mixing together the ingredients. Add to the roasting tin and turn the chicken and vegetables until they are coated. Cook for a further 5 minutes. Serve it with rice or baked potatoes, and a simple salad or green vegetables.

Preparation time:
20 minutes

Cooking time:
40 minutes

Serves: **4**

3 tablespoons olive oil
8 skinless chicken thighs
1 large lemon, cut into 8 and seeds removed
4 garlic cloves, sliced
1 tablespoon plain flour
300 ml (1/2 pint) chicken stock
3 tablespoons crème fraîche
small handful of basil leaves, shredded
8–10 pitted black olives
salt and pepper

TO SERVE:
rice or couscous
green salad

Heat the oil in a large saucepan or flameproof casserole. Add the chicken and fry gently for 5 minutes or until pale golden. Add the lemon wedges and garlic and fry for 2 minutes. Take out the lemon wedges and cut them into slices; set aside.

Add the flour to the pan and cook, stirring, for 1 minute. Stir in the stock and return the lemon slices to the pan. Bring just to the boil, reduce the heat, cover the pan and simmer gently for 30 minutes or until the chicken is cooked through. Check the seasoning.

Stir in the crème fraîche, shredded basil and olives. Heat through for 1 minute before serving with rice or couscous and a green salad.

COOK'S NOTES This dish will freeze well. Transfer to a freezer container before you add the crème fraîche, shredded basil and olives and freeze for up to 3 months. The olives and basil are stirred in shortly before serving, so it's easy to exclude them for children who aren't keen on their distinctive flavours.

99 Oriental chicken

100 One-pan chicken

Preparation time:	**2 tablespoons hoisin sauce**
15 minutes, plus	**2 tablespoons soy sauce**
marinating	**2 tablespoons sunflower oil**
	4 boneless, skinless chicken breasts,
	about 625 g (1¼ lb) in total
Cooking time:	**200 g (7 oz) broccoli**
10–15 minutes	**200 g (7 oz) long-grain white rice**
	125 g (4 oz) frozen peas
Serves: **4**	**thin strips red pepper or carrot, to**
	garnish (optional)

Mix together the hoisin sauce, soy sauce and oil in a shallow non-metallic dish. Rinse the chicken with cold water, drain well and add to dish. Spoon over the hoisin mixture, then turn over the chicken and spread the mixture over the second side. Set aside for 15 minutes.

Cut the broccoli into tiny florets and slice the stems.

Half-fill the saucepan with cold water, bring to the boil and add the rice. Cook for 6 minutes. Add the broccoli and peas and cook for a further 4 minutes.

Put the chicken breasts in a foil-lined grill pan and cook under a preheated grill for 10 minutes, turning once or twice until evenly browned and cooked through.

Cut the chicken into thick slices. Drain the rice, spoon on to serving plates and top with the chicken slices. Garnish with thin slices of red pepper or carrot, if liked.

Preparation time:	**4 chicken thighs and 4 chicken**
20 minutes	**drumsticks**
	1 kg (2 lb) baby new potatoes, large ones
Cooking time:	**halved**
1 hour	**1 small butternut squash, peeled,**
	deseeded and thickly sliced
Oven temperature:	**1 red pepper, cored, deseeded and cut**
200°C (400°F), Gas Mark 6	**into chunks**
	4 tablespoons olive oil
Serves: **4**	**1 whole garlic bulb, separated and**
	unpeeled
	few stems of sage
	1 teaspoon ground Cajun spice
	4 teaspoons clear honey
	salt and pepper

Rinse the chicken and pat dry on kitchen paper. Make 2–3 cuts in each piece and put them in a roasting tin.

Put all the vegetables in the roasting tin, spoon over the oil and add the garlic cloves. Sprinkle with a few sage leaves, salt and pepper and the Cajun spice.

Roast in a preheated oven, 200°C (400°F), Gas Mark 6, for 45 minutes. Turn the chicken, spoon the juices over the potatoes and drizzle over the honey. Cook for 15 more minutes or until the chicken is thoroughly cooked. Serve immediately.

COOK'S NOTES Make sure the chicken is cooked by inserting a skewer into one of the thickest parts. The meat should look all the same colour with no hint of pink juices. Cajun spice is available in some supermarkets in a mill ready to grind.

101 Cod parcels with hot tabbouleh

102 Plaice with pepperoni

Preparation time: **15 minutes**	**2 cod fillets, skinned**
	8 tablespoons lemon juice
	2 tablespoons extra virgin olive oil
Cooking time: **40 minutes**	**2 garlic cloves, finely chopped**
	1 teaspoon finely chopped fresh root ginger
Oven temperature: **180°C (350°F), Gas Mark 4**	**75 g (3 oz) millet**
	1 teaspoon vegetable bouillon powder
	2 tomatoes, skinned, deseeded and chopped
Serves: **2**	**1 spring onion, trimmed and sliced**
	1 teaspoon clear honey
	1 tablespoon chopped parsley

Place each cod fillet on a piece of greaseproof paper, large enough to wrap it up. Sprinkle each fillet with 1 teaspoon lemon juice, a little oil, a little garlic and 1/2 teaspoon chopped ginger. Fold and seal the edges of the greaseproof paper to form airtight parcels, being careful to allow some space above the fish.

Arrange the parcels on a baking sheet with a little cold water in the bottom and bake in a preheated oven, 180°C (350°F), Gas Mark 4, for 20 minutes or until the cod is firm to the touch. The fish will steam in its own juices.

Meanwhile, put the millet in a small saucepan with about 175 ml (6 fl oz) cold water and the bouillon powder. Bring to the boil and simmer for 20 minutes, or until the millet is cooked.

Make the dressing. Put the remaining lemon juice, oil and garlic in a food processor or blender with the tomatoes, spring onion and honey and blend until smooth.

Drain the millet and transfer it to a bowl. Add the dressing and parsley and mix well. Serve immediately with the cod fillets.

Preparation time: **10 minutes**	**8 skinless plaice fillets**
	1 small onion or shallot, finely chopped
	3 tomatoes, thinly sliced
Cooking time: **25–30 minutes**	**40 g (1 1/2 oz) pepperoni, thinly sliced**
	2 tablespoons chopped flat leaf parsley
	1 tablespoon olive oil
Oven temperature: **180°C (350°F), Gas Mark 4**	**25 g (1 oz) breadcrumbs**
	25 g (1 oz) Parmesan cheese, grated
	salt and pepper
Serves: **4**	

TO GARNISH:
flat leaf parsley sprigs
lime or lemon wedges

TO SERVE:
new potatoes
green salad

Lay 4 plaice fillets in a shallow, lightly buttered, ovenproof dish. Season lightly and scatter over the onion, then the tomato and pepperoni slices. Sprinkle with the parsley and cover with the remaining fillets.

Heat the oil in a small, nonstick frying pan and fry the breadcrumbs until pale golden. Scatter the breadcrumbs and cheese over the fish.

Bake in a preheated oven, 180°C (350°F), Gas Mark 4, for 20–25 minutes or until the fish is cooked through.

Serve the fish garnished with parsley and lime or lemon wedges and accompanied with new potatoes and a green salad.

COOK'S NOTES If plaice isn't available buy 4 cod or haddock steaks, top them with the stuffing mixture, before adding the breadcrumbs and cheese.

103 Fish burgers with yogurt mayo

104 Pasta with tuna salad

Preparation time: **15 minutes**

Cooking time: **6 minutes**

Serves: **4**

500 g (1 lb) skinless cod or haddock fillet
4 spring onions, trimmed and roughly chopped
1 egg white
50 g (2 oz) white breadcrumbs
2 tablespoons sunflower or vegetable oil
salt and pepper

TO SERVE:
3 tablespoons Greek yogurt
3 tablespoons mayonnaise
4 grainy buns
salad leaves

Preparation time: **10 minutes**

Cooking time: **10–12 minutes**

Serves: **3–4**

200 g (7 oz) can tuna in olive oil
3 tablespoons pine nuts
3 tablespoons grated Parmesan cheese
3 tablespoons extra virgin olive oil
325 g (11 oz) dried tagliatelle
200 g (7 oz) frozen sweetcorn
salt and pepper

NUTTY SALAD:
200 g (7 oz) mangetout, finely sliced
200 g (7 oz) cucumber, finely sliced
2 hard-boiled eggs, shelled and quartered
25 g (1 oz) walnuts, finely chopped
1 tablespoon walnut oil
squeeze of lemon juice

TO SERVE (OPTIONAL):
finely chopped parsley
snipped chives

Remove any remaining bones from the fish and cut it into pieces. Put the fish in a food processor or blender with the spring onions and process briefly until the ingredients are finely chopped. Add the egg white, breadcrumbs and a little salt and pepper and process briefly until the ingredients are combined.

Divide the mixture into 4 and use dampened hands to shape each portion into a flat burger.

Heat the oil in a nonstick frying pan and fry the burgers for about 3 minutes on each side until golden and firm.

Meanwhile, mix together the yogurt, mayonnaise and a little salt and pepper. Split the buns and pile salad leaves on to each base. Put the burgers on top of the salad and add a spoonful of yogurt mayonnaise. Sandwich together with the burger tops and serve.

COOK'S NOTES **To make a more substantial meal serve the fish burgers with a salad and oven-baked jacket chips. If you like, flavour the yogurt mayonnaise with finely chopped fresh herbs, such as tarragon, fresh coriander or dill.**

Put the tuna and its oil in a food processor or blender with the nuts and cheese. Add pepper to taste. Blend to a purée while gradually adding the oil.

Cook the pasta in lightly salted boiling water according to the instructions on the packet. About 2 minutes before the pasta is just cooked add the sweetcorn.

Meanwhile, make the salad. Put the mangetout, cucumber, eggs and walnuts in a bowl. Just before serving, add the walnut oil and lemon juice and toss.

When the pasta and sweetcorn are cooked, add about 250 ml (8 fl oz) water from the pasta to the tuna sauce. Blend until smooth. Drain the pasta and sweetcorn, turn into a warm bowl and pour the sauce over. Sprinkle with the herbs (if used) and serve immediately.

105 Creamy fish pie

106 Savoury fish pie

Preparation time: **20 minutes**	**4 small baking potatoes, about 500 g (1 lb) in total, cut into large chunks** **1 small leek, diced**
Cooking time: **about 50 minutes**	**1 large salmon steak, about 250 g (8 oz)** **1 cod steak, about 200 g (7 oz)** **300 ml (½ pint) semi-skimmed milk**
Oven temperature: **200°C (400°F), Gas Mark 6**	**50 g (2 oz) butter** **25 g (1 oz) plain flour** **grated rind and juice of ½ lemon**
Serves: **2**	**2 tablespoons chopped parsley, plus extra to garnish** **salt and pepper**

Cook the potatoes in lightly salted boiling water for 15 minutes or until tender. Steam the leek for 4–5 minutes or until tender.

Meanwhile, put the salmon and cod in a saucepan with the milk. Bring to the boil, reduce the heat and simmer for 5 minutes. Remove from the heat and leave to cool for a few minutes. Lift the fish out of the milk, peel away the skin and flake the fish into large pieces. Carefully check for any bones and then set aside, reserving the milk.

Melt half the butter and stir in the flour. Gradually add the reserved milk and bring to the boil, stirring until thickened and smooth. Add the lemon rind and parsley and season with salt and pepper, then carefully stir in the flaked fish. Spoon the fish mixture into a 900 ml (1½ pint) ovenproof dish.

Drain and mash the potatoes, then beat in the leek and lemon juice. Season to taste and spoon the mash over the fish mixture and dot with the remaining butter. Cook in a preheated oven, 200°C (400°F), Gas Mark 6, for 25 minutes or until the top is golden. Garnish with extra parsley and serve.

Preparation time: **25 minutes**	**750 g (1½ lb) potatoes, thinly sliced** **750 g (1½ lb) cod or haddock fillet** **350 ml (12 fl oz) semi-skimmed milk**
Cooking time: **about 1¼ hours**	**25 g (1 oz) butter** **500 g (1 lb) leeks, sliced** **2 tablespoons plain white flour**
Oven temperature: **180°C (350°F), Gas Mark 4**	**125 g (4 oz) blue cheese, crumbled** **plenty of grated nutmeg** **salt and pepper**
Serves: **4–5**	**watercress, to garnish**

Cook the potatoes in lightly salted boiling water for 8–10 minutes or until tender. Drain.

Meanwhile, put the fish in a large, nonstick frying pan and pour on one-third of the milk. Cover the pan and simmer gently for 6–8 minutes or until cooked through. Transfer the fish to a plate and reserve the cooking liquid.

Melt the butter in a clean pan, add the leeks and cook until softened. Stir in the flour and cook, stirring, for 1 minute. Gradually blend in the reserved liquid and remaining milk, whisking until the sauce has thickened. Add the cheese and stir until melted. Season with nutmeg, salt and pepper.

Roughly flake the fish, removing any stray bones and pour on half of the sauce. Layer the potato slices over the filling and pour on the remaining sauce. Bake in a preheated oven, 180°C (350°F), Gas Mark 4, for about 50 minutes or until golden and bubbling. Serve garnished with watercress.

COOK'S NOTES Accentuate the golden topping by sprinkling over 2 tablespoons grated Cheddar and a little finely crumbled blue cheese before baking.

107 North African fish stew

Preparation time:
15 minutes

Cooking time:
15 minutes

Serves: **4–6**

3 tablespoons olive oil
500 g (1 lb) cod or haddock fillet, skinned and cut in chunks
250 g (8 oz) squid rings
2 small red onions, chopped
1 small fennel bulb or 2 celery sticks, chopped
3 garlic cloves, sliced
2 tablespoons paprika
1 tablespoon cumin seeds
¹/₂ teaspoon dried chilli flakes
4 tablespoons sun-dried tomato paste
900 ml (1¹/₂ pints) fish or vegetable stock
400 g (13 oz) can black beans or red kidney beans, rinsed and drained

TO SERVE:
small handful of fresh coriander leaves
small handful of mint sprigs
rice or wholegrain bread

Heat the oil in a large, nonstick frying pan, add the white fish and squid rings and fry gently for 2 minutes. Remove the fish with a slotted spoon and set aside.

Add the onions, fennel or celery, garlic and spices to the pan and fry for 3 minutes. Add the tomato paste, stock and beans. Bring just to the boil, add the fish and simmer gently for 10 minutes or until piping hot.

Meanwhile, roughly chop the herbs. Serve the fish stew in warm bowls, sprinkled with the herbs, and with rice or wholegrain bread to soak up the juice.

108 Tuna kedgeree

Preparation time:
10 minutes

Cooking time:
about 15 minutes

Serves: **4**

250 g (8 oz) basmati rice
100 g (3¹/₂ oz) frozen baby broad beans
400 g (13 oz) can tuna in oil or brine, drained
25 g (1 oz) unsalted butter
1 small onion, finely chopped
1 teaspoon medium curry paste
4 eggs, hard-boiled, shelled and cut in wedges
small handful of flat leaf parsley, chopped, plus extra sprigs to garnish
salt and pepper
lemon or lime wedges, to serve

Cook the rice in plenty of lightly salted boiling water for about 8 minutes or until almost tender. Add the broad beans, cook for a further 3 minutes and drain.

Flake the tuna into small chunks. Melt the butter in a large, nonstick frying pan, add the onion and curry paste and fry gently for 3 minutes. Add the drained rice and broad beans, with the tuna and eggs.

Stir in the parsley and season the kedgeree with salt and pepper. Stir gently over a low heat for 1 minute, then transfer to warm serving plates. Garnish with parsley and serve with lemon or lime wedges.

COOK'S NOTES Use frozen sweetcorn or peas instead of broad beans if you prefer. Canned tuna is such a useful storecupboard standby, not just as a sandwich filler, but for adding to pies, pizza toppings and baked potatoes. Here it successfully takes the place of the more usual smoked haddock.

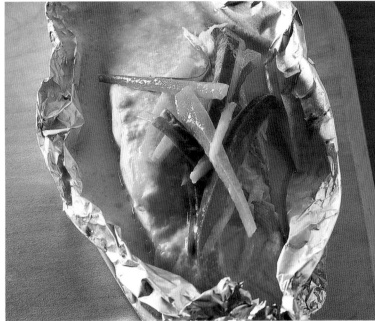

Preparation time: **10 minutes**	**325 g (11 oz) dried penne or other pasta shapes**
	2 tablespoons olive oil
Cooking time: **15 minutes**	**1 onion, thinly sliced**
	400 g (13 oz) can red or pink salmon
	150 g (5 oz) frozen peas
Serves: **4**	**2 tablespoons pesto**
	1 tablespoon lemon juice
	25 g (1 oz) Parmesan cheese, grated, plus shavings to garnish
	salt and pepper
	green salad, to serve (optional)

Cook the pasta for 8–10 minutes or according to the instructions on the packet.

Meanwhile, heat the oil in a nonstick frying pan, add the onion and fry for about 5 minutes or until softened. Drain the salmon and discard any skin and bones. Roughly flake the flesh with a fork.

Add the peas to the pasta and cook for a further 3 minutes. Drain the pasta and peas, reserving a few tablespoonfuls of the cooking liquid, and return to the pan.

Stir in the pesto, lemon juice, cheese, onion and flaked salmon. Season lightly with salt and pepper and toss gently. Serve immediately, topped with Parmesan shavings and accompanied by a leafy salad, if liked.

COOK'S NOTES Canned salmon might not taste as good as its fresh counterpart, but it's ideal for creating an easy meal. Bottled pesto sauce is another valuable storecupboard standby. For this recipe, use either the familiar green pesto, made from basil and Parmesan, or red pesto, flavoured with peppers and tomatoes. For a milder flavour use Cheddar cheese instead of Parmesan.

Preparation time: **20 minutes**	**4 salmon fillets, about 625 g (1¼ lb) in total**
	juice of 1½ limes
Cooking time: **10 minutes**	**2 carrots, cut in thin strips**
	4 spring onions, trimmed and cut into strips
Oven temperature: **180°C (350°F), Gas Mark 4**	**1 small red pepper, cored and deseeded**
	2.5 cm (1 inch) fresh root ginger, peeled and grated
Serves: **4**	**150 g (5 oz) coconut milk**
	200 g (7 oz) basmati or jasmine rice
	6 tablespoons chopped fresh coriander, plus extra sprigs to garnish
	salt and pepper

Rinse the salmon in cold water, drain and put each piece on a separate piece of foil, skin down. Season with salt and pepper and fold up the edges of the foil. Squeeze the juice of ½ lime over the salmon.

Divide the vegetables and ginger among the parcels. Spoon 3 tablespoons coconut milk and 1 tablespoon water around each piece of salmon. Fold up the edges of the foil to make a parcel and put them on a baking sheet. Cook in a preheated oven, 180°C (350°F), Gas Mark 4, for 10 minutes.

Meanwhile, cook the rice in boiling water for 8–10 minutes or until tender. Drain the rice into the sieve, then tip it back into the dry pan.

Add the chopped coriander and the juice of 1 lime to the rice, season with salt and pepper, stir to mix and spoon on to serving plates.

Carefully open the parcels and arrange the salmon, vegetables and coconut juices on top of the rice. Garnish with sprigs of coriander and serve immediately.

111 Mixed fish skewers　　112 Tuna fishcakes

Preparation time: 15 minutes	300 g (10 oz) salmon fillet, skinned 300 g (10 oz) haddock fillet, skinned 2 tablespoons lemon juice
Cooking time: 6 minutes	3 teaspoons Dijon mustard 2 teaspoons muscovado sugar 3 tablespoons olive oil
Serves: 4	200 g (7 oz) crème fraîche 2 teaspoons chopped dill few cos lettuce leaves salt and pepper lemon wedges, to serve (optional)

Rinse and drain the fish and cut the flesh into 2 cm (³/₄ inch) cubes. Thread alternate colours of fish on to 8 small skewers. Arrange the skewers in a foil-lined grill pan.

In a small bowl mix together the lemon juice with 2 teaspoons mustard, the sugar, oil and a little salt and pepper. Spoon half the mixture over the fish.

Cook the fish skewers under a preheated grill for 3 minutes. Turn the skewers and spoon over the rest of the oil mixture. Grill for 3 more minutes or until the fish breaks easily when pressed with a knife.

Meanwhile, mix the rest of the mustard with the crème fraîche. Add the dill and season with some salt and pepper. Spoon into another small bowl.

Arrange the lettuce on serving plates. Top with 2 skewers and serve with lemon wedges, if liked, and spoonfuls of sauce.

Preparation time: 15 minutes	425 g (14 oz) potatoes, halved 125 g (4 oz) broccoli 50 g (2 oz) frozen peas
Cooking time: 20–25 minutes	rind and juice of ¹/₂ lemon 25 g (1 oz) butter 2 x 200 g (7 oz) cans tuna in water or oil, 　drained
Makes: 8 fishcakes	125 g (4 oz) sliced bread 2 eggs, beaten 4 teaspoons chopped mint 150 ml (5 fl oz) natural yogurt 4 tablespoons sunflower oil salt and pepper salad, to serve

Cook the potatoes in boiling water for 10 minutes. Cut the broccoli into florets and the stems into slices. Add to the top of the steamer, cover and cook for 5 minutes. Add the peas for the last 3 minutes.

Drain the potatoes and return to the dry pan with half the lemon rind, all the juice, the butter and a little salt and pepper. Mash until smooth.

Mix the tuna into the potato together with the broccoli and peas. When the mixture is cool enough to handle divide it into 8 and shape the portions into rounds.

Tear the bread into pieces, put into a food processor or blender and process into fine crumbs. Tip into a shallow bowl. Coat the fishcakes in egg, then in breadcrumbs.

Meanwhile, mix the mint with the yogurt, remaining lemon rind and a little salt and pepper.

Heat half the oil in a large, nonstick frying pan. Add 4 fishcakes and fry for 5–6 minutes, turning once until golden on both sides. Cook the remaining fishcakes in the same way. Serve with the yogurt sauce and salad.

5 Vegetarian

113 Spicy tofu burgers with cucumber relish

114 Smoked tofu and apricot sausages

Preparation time:
15 minutes

Cooking time:
15 minutes

Serves: **4**

4 tablespoons soya or groundnut oil
1 small red onion, finely chopped
1 celery stick, finely chopped
2 garlic cloves, crushed
200 g (7 oz) can red kidney beans
75 g (3 oz) salted peanuts
250 g (8 oz) tofu
2 teaspoons medium curry paste
50 g (2 oz) breadcrumbs
1 egg
¹/₂ small cucumber, peeled and deseeded
2 tablespoons chopped flat leaf parsley
1 tablespoon white wine vinegar
2 teaspoons caster sugar

Preparation time:
20 minutes

Cooking time:
10 minutes

Serves: **4**

220 g (7¹/₂ oz) smoked tofu
2 tablespoons olive or soya oil, plus extra
for frying
1 large onion, roughly chopped
2 celery sticks, roughly chopped
100 g (3¹/₂ oz) no-soak dried apricots,
roughly chopped
50 g (2 oz) breadcrumbs
1 egg
1 tablespoon chopped sage
salt and pepper
relish and potato wedges, to serve

Heat 1 tablespoon oil in a nonstick frying pan and gently fry all but 1 tablespoon onion with the celery for 5 minutes or until they are soft. Add the garlic and fry for a further 2 minutes.

Put the kidney beans in a bowl and mash them lightly to break them up. Finely chop the peanuts in a food processor. Pat the tofu dry on kitchen paper, break it into pieces and add it to the nuts in the food processor or blender. Blend them until the tofu is crumbly, then add the mixture to the beans together with the fried vegetables, curry paste, breadcrumbs and egg. Mix everything well to obtain a thick paste.

Divide the mixture into 4 and shape into burgers, dusting your hands with flour if the mixture is sticky. Heat the remaining oil in the pan and gently fry the burgers for about 4 minutes on each side or until golden.

Meanwhile, chop the cucumber finely and mix it with the reserved tablespoon of onion, the parsley, vinegar and sugar in a small bowl. Serve with the burgers.

COOK'S NOTES Red kidney beans add colour and texture to these chunky burgers, but other cooked beans, such as soya beans, would work just as well.

Pat the tofu dry on kitchen paper and tear into chunks. Heat the oil in a nonstick frying pan and cook the onion and celery for 5 minutes or until they are softened. Transfer to a food processor and add the tofu and apricots. Blend the ingredients to a chunky paste, scraping down the mixture from the sides of the bowl if necessary.

Tip the mixture into a bowl and add the breadcrumbs, egg and sage. Season with salt and pepper and mix to combine.

Divide the mixture into 8 and shape each portion into a sausage, pressing the mixture together firmly and dusting your hands with flour if the mixture is sticky.

Heat a little oil in a frying pan, preferably nonstick, and fry the sausages for about 5 minutes or until they are golden. Serve immediately with a spicy relish and potato wedges, if liked.

115 Tomato ratatouille gratin

116 Cashew and oriental stir fry

Preparation time:
15 minutes

Cooking time:
1 hour

Oven temperature:
220°C (425°F), Gas Mark 7

Serves: **4–6**

4 tablespoons olive oil
2 onions, finely chopped
2 garlic cloves, crushed (optional)
1 aubergine, diced
500 g (1 lb) courgettes, diced
3 red peppers, deseeded and roughly chopped
1 yellow pepper, deseeded and roughly chopped
2 green peppers, deseeded and roughly chopped
2 x 425 g (14 oz) cans chopped tomatoes
2 teaspoons dried mixed herbs
50 g (2 oz) dried breadcrumbs
25 g (1 oz) Cheddar cheese, grated
1 tablespoon grated Parmesan cheese
salt and pepper
green salad, to serve

Preparation time:
15 minutes

Cooking time:
6 minutes

Serves: **4–6**

2 tablespoons vegetable oil
1 green pepper, deseeded and finely sliced
2 red peppers, deseeded and finely sliced
1 red onion, finely sliced
2 carrots, sliced or cut into strips
125 g (4 oz) choi sum or green cabbage, shredded
175 g (6 oz) bean sprouts
2 tablespoons hoisin sauce
2–3 tablespoons soy sauce or tamari sauce
5 tablespoons water
75 g (3 oz) cashew nuts, toasted
1 tablespoon sesame seeds, toasted
handful of fresh coriander leaves
rice or noodles, to serve

Heat the oil in a large, nonstick frying pan and fry the onions until they are soft and golden-brown. Add the garlic (if used) and cook for a further minute.

Add the aubergine and courgettes to the pan and cook on all sides until softened and beginning to brown. Add the chopped peppers to the pan and stir to coat in the oil. Simmer for 5 minutes or until the peppers have softened.

Add the tomatoes and bring to the boil. Reduce the heat, season to taste and add the dried mixed herbs, half cover the pan with a lid and simmer for 10 minutes.

Spoon the mixture into a large ovenproof dish and level the top. Mix the breadcrumbs with the cheeses and sprinkle on top. Bake in a preheated oven, 220°C (425°F), Gas Mark 7, for 20–25 minutes or until the breadcrumb mixture is golden-brown and bubbling. Serve with a green salad.

Heat the oil in a wok or large, nonstick frying pan and fry the peppers, onion, carrots, choi sum and bean sprouts. Stir-fry over a high heat for 3–4 minutes or until piping hot.

Mix the hoisin and soy sauces (or tamari sauce) with the water and add to the pan. Stir-fry for a further 1 minute.

Add the cashew nuts and sesame seeds and toss together. Add the coriander leaves and serve immediately with rice or egg noodles.

117 Go faster pasta

Preparation time: **15 minutes**	**500 g (1 lb) tubular pasta, such as penne or rigatoni grated Parmesan cheese, to serve**
Cooking time: **20 minutes**	TOMATO SAUCE: **5 tablespoons extra virgin olive oil 1 onion, finely chopped 1 celery stick, finely chopped 2 garlic cloves, crushed 1 kg (2 lb) tomatoes, skinned, deseeded and finely chopped or 2 x 400 g (13 oz) cans Italian plum tomatoes 12 basil leaves 1 teaspoon raw brown sugar salt and pepper**
Serves: **4**	

Make the sauce. Heat the oil in a large, nonstick pan and slowly sauté the onion and celery until they are soft. Add the garlic, tomatoes, basil and sugar and cook briskly over a high heat for 10 minutes.

Leave the sauce to cool, then blend in a food processor or blender until smooth. Return the sauce to the pan and simmer for 10 minutes. Season to taste.

Meanwhile, cook the pasta in boiling water for about 10 minutes or according to the instructions on the packet. Drain well and toss with the tomato sauce. Serve with grated Parmesan.

COOK'S NOTES Substitute corn, rice, vegetable or millet pasta for wheat pasta if your child is allergic to wheat or gluten. The sauce can be made in advance and frozen to save time.

118 Tomato and red pepper pasta

Preparation time: **15 minutes**	**200 g (7 oz) linguine or pasta twists 1 tablespoon olive oil 1 onion, chopped 400 g (13 oz) jar red pimientos, drained and diced 5 pieces sun-dried tomatoes, drained and finely sliced 1–2 garlic cloves, crushed 400 g (13 oz) can chopped tomatoes 150 ml (1/4 pint) vegetable or chicken stock 2 teaspoons caster sugar 3 tablespoons double cream (optional) a little grated Parmesan cheese or shavings few basil leaves (optional) salt and pepper**
Cooking time: **20 minutes**	
Serves: **4**	

Cook the pasta in boiling water for about 10 minutes or according to the instructions on the packet.

Meanwhile, heat the oil in a large, nonstick frying pan, add the onion and fry, stirring occasionally, for 5 minutes or until the onion is pale golden. Add the pimientos, sun-dried tomatoes and garlic to the onion. Fry for 2 more minutes, then add the canned tomatoes, stock and sugar. Season to taste. Cook gently, stirring occasionally, for 10 minutes.

Drain the pasta, tip it back into a dry pan and stir in the tomato sauce and the cream (if used). Toss together, spoon into warm bowls and serve topped with Parmesan cheese and basil leaves (if used).

119 Falafel

120 Vegetable chips with pumpkin dip

Preparation time:
15 minutes, plus soaking

Cooking time:
about 2 hours

Makes:
12–16 falafels

125 g (4 oz) dried chickpeas, soaked overnight
25 g (1 oz) bulgar wheat
1 large onion, roughly chopped
2 garlic cloves, roughly chopped
4 tablespoons chopped parsley
1 teaspoon cumin seeds, crushed
1 teaspoon coriander seeds, crushed
1/2 teaspoon baking powder
4 tablespoons extra virgin olive oil
salt and pepper

TO SERVE:
pitta bread
green salad
Greek yogurt

Preparation time:
15 minutes

Cooking time:
20 minutes

Oven temperature:
200°C (400°F), Gas Mark 6

Serves: **4**

1 large baking potato
2 parsnips
1 sweet potato
2 carrots
250 g (8 oz) celeriac
1 large uncooked beetroot
3–4 tablespoons olive oil

PUMPKIN DIP:
175 g (6 oz) pumpkin seeds
2 garlic cloves, finely chopped
3–5 spring onions, trimmed and sliced
1/2 teaspoon ground cumin
3 large tomatoes, skinned, deseeded and diced
juice of 1/2 lime
3 tablespoons tomato purée

Drain the chickpeas, place them in a saucepan and cover with plenty of fresh water. Bring to the boil and boil for 10 minutes. Reduce the heat and simmer for 1–1 1/2 hours until they are soft. Drain. Meanwhile, soak the bulgar wheat in warm water for 1 hour. Drain.

Put the chickpeas, bulgar wheat, onion, garlic, parsley, cumin, coriander and baking powder in a food processor or blender. Season to taste and process until the mixture forms a firm paste. Shape into walnut-sized balls and flatten slightly.

Put the oil in a deep, heavy-based frying pan and heat it until a small piece of the falafel mixture sizzles. Fry the falafels in batches until golden. Drain on kitchen paper and serve warm with wholemeal pitta bread, a large green salad and some Greek yogurt.

COOK'S NOTES The falafels can be frozen after being shaped. Put on a baking sheet lined with clingfilm and freeze for 30 minutes or until hard, then transfer to a freezer bag. They can be stored for up to 4 weeks. To cook, defrost at room temperature for 1–2 hours and fry.

Cut all the vegetables into strips about 1 cm (1/2 inch) thick. Put the oil in a large baking tin and heat in a preheated oven, 200°C (400°F), Gas Mark 6, until hot. Add the vegetable chips to the baking tin, making sure they are all covered in oil. Return the tin to the oven and cook for 20 minutes or until the chips are lightly browned on the outside and soft on the inside. Keep checking and shaking the tray while they are cooking.

Meanwhile, make the pumpkin dip. Dry-fry the pumpkin seeds in a frying pan over a moderate heat for 5–10 minutes. Shake the pan and turn them as they pop and go golden-brown. Remove the pan from the heat and allow to cool. Grind the seeds coarsely in a spice grinder or food processor. Add the garlic, spring onions, ground cumin, tomatoes, lime juice and tomato purée and blend together until the mixture becomes quite smooth.

Serve with the dip in a separate bowl with the vegetables as dippers.

121 Cowboy beans

122 Veggie puff pie

Preparation time: **15 minutes, plus soaking**	**175 g (6 oz) dried pinto, borlotti or** **cannellini beans, soaked overnight** **1 bay leaf**
Cooking time: **1¼ hours**	**1 tablespoon olive oil** **1 onion, finely chopped** **1 garlic clove, crushed**
Serves: **4**	**1 tablespoon plain flour** **1 teaspoon paprika** **300 ml (½ pint) vegetable stock** **1 tablespoon tomato purée** **1 tablespoon brown sugar** **1 teaspoon Dijon mustard (optional)** **salt and pepper** **warm bread, to serve**

SLAW:
1 small banana, sliced
1 small orange, separated into segments
1 small dessert apple, cored and diced
75 g (3 oz) red cabbage, cored and finely
   shredded
3 tablespoons sprouted alfalfa seeds,
   rinsed

Drain the beans, rinse and transfer to a saucepan with the bay leaf. Cover with cold water, bring to the boil and boil rapidly for 10 minutes. Skim off any scum and simmer for 1 hour or until tender.

Heat the olive oil in a large, nonstick frying pan, add the onion and garlic and fry, stirring, for 5 minutes or until golden. Stir in the flour and paprika and cook for 1 minute, then stir in the stock, tomato purée, sugar and mustard (if used). Season to taste. Meanwhile, toss all the slaw ingredients together in a bowl.

Drain the beans, return to the saucepan and stir in the sauce. Bring to the boil, cover and simmer for 15 minutes. Spoon into warm serving bowls, top with the slaw and serve with warm bread.

Preparation time: **15 minutes**	**100 g (3½ oz) cashew nuts** **3 tablespoons olive oil** **1 leek, about 250 g (8 oz), thinly sliced**
Cooking time: **about 25 minutes**	**250 g (8 oz) button mushrooms, quartered** **1 tablespoon plain flour** **450 ml (¾ pint) full-fat milk**
Oven temperature: **200°C (400°F), Gas Mark 6**	**375 g (12 oz) puff pastry (thawed if frozen)** **beaten egg, to glaze** **salt and pepper**
Serves: **4**	

Scatter the cashew nuts over the bottom of a foil-lined grill pan and toast briefly under a hot grill, turning frequently, until golden. Turn into a blender, add 2 tablespoons oil and work to a smooth paste.

Heat the remaining oil in a nonstick frying pan, add the leek and mushrooms and fry, stirring, for 3–4 minutes or until lightly browned. Stir in the flour, then add the nut paste and gradually mix in the milk. Bring to the boil, stirring. Season to taste and spoon into a 1.2 litre (2 pint) pie dish.

Roll out the pastry on a lightly floured surface until it is 5 cm (2 inches) larger all round than the top of the pie dish. Cut off a 1 cm (½ inch) wide strip of pastry from around the edge. Moisten the rim of the pie dish with a little water and position the pastry strip on the rim. Brush with beaten egg, then lift the pastry lid into position.

Press the pastry edges together, trim off excess and decorate the top with off-cuts. Brush the top of the pie with egg and bake in a preheated oven, 200°C (400°F), Gas Mark 6, for about 20 minutes or until well risen and golden. Serve immediately.

COOK'S NOTES Although there isn't any cream in this tasty filling, finely ground cashew nuts add a lovely richness to the sauce. Get the children to help you decorate the pie top, adding pastry numerals or their initials.

123 Lentil thatch

Preparation time:
15 minutes

Cooking time:
about 55 minutes

Oven temperature:
200°C (400°F), Gas Mark 6

Serves: **4**

1 tablespoon sunflower oil
1 onion, finely chopped
2 carrots, about 175 g (6 oz) in total, diced
2 celery sticks, sliced
1 garlic clove, crushed
100 g (3¹/₂ oz) red lentils, rinsed
900 ml (1¹/₂ pints) vegetable stock
2 teaspoons tomato purée
625 g (1¹/₄ lb) potatoes, cut into chunks
3 tablespoons full-fat milk
40 g (1¹/₂ oz) butter
salt and pepper

TO FINISH (OPTIONAL):
2 carrots, sliced lengthways
1 red pepper, cored and deseeded
4 frozen peas, defrosted

Heat the oil in a large, nonstick pan, add the onion and fry for 4–5 minutes or until lightly browned. Add the carrots, celery and garlic, cook for 1 minute, then stir in the lentils, stock and tomato purée. Add salt and pepper to taste. Bring to the boil and simmer uncovered, stirring occasionally, for 30 minutes or until the lentils are soft.

Meanwhile, cook the potatoes in a separate pan for 15 minutes or until tender. Drain and mash with the milk and half of the butter. Add salt and pepper to taste.

Spoon the lentil mixture into 4 square, ovenproof dishes, each holding 300 ml (¹/₂ pint). Top with the mashed potato, dot with the remaining butter and bake in a preheated oven, 200°C (400°F), Gas Mark 6, for 20 minutes or until piping hot.

To finish, if liked add raw carrot roof tiles, red pepper windows and door, a pea doorknob and carrot strips to mark the window panes. Serve hot.

124 Red pepper and polenta bake

Preparation time:
15 minutes

Cooking time:
about 40 minutes

Oven temperature:
200°C (400°F), Gas Mark 6

Serves: **4**

500 ml (17 fl oz) water
125 g (4 oz) instant polenta
125 g (4 oz) medium Cheddar cheese, grated
25 g (1 oz) butter
5 teaspoons olive oil
1 onion, finely chopped
1 red pepper, cored, deseeded and cut into large squares
375 g (12 oz) butternut squash, deseeded, peeled and cut into large cubes
1 garlic clove, crushed
400 g (13 oz) can chopped tomatoes
150 ml (¹/₄ pint) vegetable stock
2 teaspoons finely chopped rosemary (optional)
salt and pepper
green beans, to serve

Bring the measured water to the boil in a saucepan and add the polenta in a steady stream, stirring continually. Cook, stirring, until the polenta is thick and smooth. Take off the heat. Reserve a little cheese for the topping and stir the rest into the polenta with the butter and a little salt and pepper. Spoon the polenta into a shallow, oiled rectangular dish, about 18 x 28 x 4 cm (7 x 11 x 1¹/₂ inches), and leave to cool and set.

Heat 3 teaspoons oil in a saucepan, add the onion and fry, stirring, for 4–5 minutes or until lightly browned. Add the red pepper, squash and garlic and fry for 2 minutes. Stir in the tomatoes, stock, rosemary (if used) and a little seasoning. Cover and simmer for 15 minutes. Spoon into a shallow, 2 litre (3¹/₂ pint) ovenproof dish.

Loosen the polenta and turn it out on a board. Use biscuit cutters to stamp out hearts, stars or circles and arrange the shapes over the top of the pepper mixture. Brush with the remaining oil and sprinkle with cheese. Bake in a preheated oven, 200°C (400°F), Gas Mark 6, for 15 minutes. Serve immediately with steamed green beans.

125 Stripy macaroni cheese

126 Cabbage parcels with carrot sauce

Preparation time:
15 minutes

Cooking time:
about 25 minutes

Serves: **2**

125 g (4 oz) dried macaroni
100 g (3¹/₂ oz) broccoli, cut into tiny
   florets and stems sliced
1 carrot, about 125 g (4 oz), sliced
50 g (2 oz) frozen sweetcorn
15 g (¹/₂ oz) butter
15 g (¹/₂ oz) plain flour
200 ml (7 fl oz) full-fat milk
1 teaspoon Dijon mustard (optional)
100 g (3¹/₂ oz) medium Cheddar cheese,
   grated
1 tablespoon breadcrumbs
cherry tomatoes, quartered, to serve

Preparation time:
20 minutes

Cooking time:
15 minutes

Serves: **2**

150 g (5 oz) carrots, thickly sliced
400 ml (14 fl oz) hot vegetable stock
50 g (2 oz) couscous
1 tablespoon raisins
2 ready-to-eat dried apricots, chopped
¹/₄ red pepper, deseeded and diced
2 tablespoons frozen peas
pinch of ground allspice
2 teaspoons olive oil
2 Savoy cabbage leaves, thick stems
   removed
salt and pepper

Cook the macaroni in boiling water for about 10 minutes or according to the instructions on the packet.

Meanwhile, steam the broccoli, carrot and sweetcorn over a separate pan of boiling water for 6–7 minutes. Lift the steamer off the pan and keep covered.

Melt the butter in the dry steamer pan. Stir in the flour and cook for 1 minute, then gradually mix in the milk and bring to the boil, stirring, until the sauce is thick and smooth. Stir in the mustard (if used) and three-quarters of the cheese.

Drain the macaroni and stir it into the sauce. Spoon two-thirds of the macaroni cheese into 2 ovenproof dishes, each holding 200 ml (7 fl oz). Arrange the carrot, broccoli and sweetcorn in layers on top, then cover with the rest of the macaroni cheese.

Sprinkle over the remaining cheese and breadcrumbs and brown under a hot grill for 5 minutes. Set on serving plates and allow to cool slightly before serving with cherry tomatoes.

COOK'S NOTES Make this quick and easy pasta dish in heatproof glass dishes so that children can see and count the different layers.

Put the carrots and 300 ml (¹/₂ pint) stock in the base of a steamer pan and bring to the boil. Cover and simmer for 10 minutes. Meanwhile, put the couscous in a bowl, pour over the remaining hot stock and leave to soak for 5 minutes.

Add the raisins, apricots, red pepper, peas, allspice and oil to the soaked couscous, mix together and season lightly. Spoon the mixture into the cabbage leaves, folding up the sides of the leaves to encase the filling.

Put the cabbage parcels in the steamer above the carrots. Cover and cook for 5 minutes or until the cabbage is tender. Keep the steamer covered.

Purée the carrots with half of the stock until smooth. Gradually blend in enough of the remaining stock to make a pouring sauce. Spoon the sauce over the base of 2 serving plates. Place the cabbage parcels on top and serve.

COOK'S NOTES Instead of couscous you could try using bulgar wheat. Soak it in stock as above for 15 minutes before use. For a change use butternut squash in place of carrot; it makes an equally delicious, vibrant sauce.

127 Vegetable wigwams

128 Beat-the-clock pizzas

Preparation time:
15 minutes

Cooking time:
about 12 minutes

Serves: **2**

75 g (3 oz) basmati rice
75 g (3 oz) baby corn cobs, halved
  lengthways
75 g (3 oz) carrot, cut into sticks
50 g (2 oz) green beans, halved
1 teaspoon sunflower oil
1 tablespoon sesame seeds
1 teaspoon light soy sauce
40 g (1¹/₂ oz) frozen chopped spinach,
  thawed and well drained
50 g (2 oz) tofu, rinsed, drained and cut
  into small dice

Add the rice to a steamer pan part-filled with boiling water and simmer for 5 minutes. Put all the vegetables in the steamer, place it on the pan and steam for 5 minutes or until both rice and vegetables are tender.

Meanwhile, heat the oil in a small, nonstick frying pan. Add the sesame seeds and fry until lightly browned. Take the pan off the heat and add the soy sauce. Quickly cover the pan and set aside.

Drain the rice, rinse with boiling water and mix with the spinach and tofu. Add the sesame seeds to the rice.

Spoon the rice into mounds on 2 serving plates and arrange the vegetables upright around the rice to resemble a wigwam.

COOK'S NOTES **Add shredded omelette to the rice instead of tofu if you prefer. Firm tofu is available chilled in sealed packs of water or in longlife packs and holds its shape better than softer silken tofu.**

Preparation time:
20 minutes

Cooking time:
10 minutes

Oven temperature:
200°C (400°F), Gas Mark 6

Makes:
4 pizzas

250 g (8 oz) self-raising flour
50 g (2 oz) butter or block margarine,
  diced
1 egg
100 ml (3¹/₂ fl oz) full-fat milk
oil, for greasing
4 tablespoons passata
4 teaspoons chopped oregano, marjoram
  or mixed herbs
50 g (2 oz) frozen sweetcorn
50 g (2 oz) medium Cheddar or mozzarella
  cheese, grated

TO GARNISH:
2 green peppers, halved, cored and
  deseeded
1 red pepper, halved, cored and deseeded

TO SERVE (OPTIONAL):
cherry tomatoes
cucumber

Put the flour in a bowl and rub in the butter with your fingertips until the mixture resembles fine breadcrumbs. Stir in the egg and enough milk to mix to a smooth and soft, but not sticky, dough.

Knead briefly on a lightly floured surface, then divide the dough into 4 pieces. Roll out each one to a 12 cm (5 inch) circle. Place on a large, lightly oiled baking sheet and brush with passata. Sprinkle with the herbs and sweetcorn.

Top with the cheese and bake in a preheated oven, 200°C (400°F), Gas Mark 6, for 10 minutes or until well risen and the cheese has melted.

Use tiny number cutters to cut the main clock numerals from the green peppers. Cut red pepper clock hands. Arrange these on the pizzas. Serve warm, with cherry tomatoes and sliced cucumber, if liked.

129 Potato pizza

130 Broccoli, tomato and corn risotto

Preparation time:	750 g (1½ lb) potatoes, grated
20 minutes	4 tablespoons extra virgin olive oil
	4 tablespoons tomato purée
Cooking time:	1 garlic clove, crushed
30 minutes	selection of toppings, such as sliced mushrooms, sliced tomatoes,
Makes:	sweetcorn, finely sliced spring onion,
4 pizzas	olives, capers, finely chopped red and green peppers
	175 g (6 oz) goats' cheese, crumbled, or Cheddar cheese, grated
	2 teaspoons chopped oregano
	salt and pepper

Preparation time:	4 tablespoons vegetable oil
15 minutes	1 large onion, finely chopped
	3 garlic cloves, finely chopped
Cooking time:	375 g (12 oz) brown rice
35–40 minutes	1 litre (1¾ pints) hot vegetable stock
	500 g (1 lb) tomatoes, skinned and chopped
Serves: 4	250 g (8 oz) broccoli, chopped
	500 g (1 lb) frozen sweetcorn
	3–4 tablespoons finely chopped fresh coriander
	salt and pepper or vegetable bouillon powder

Squeeze the grated potato in kitchen paper to remove any excess liquid. Heat 1 tablespoon oil in a heavy-based, nonstick frying pan. Add one-quarter of the potato and flatten it to a round just smaller than the pan. Cook for 4–5 minutes on each side until the base is crisp and golden. Place on a baking sheet and repeat with the remaining potato.

Mix the tomato purée and garlic and spread it evenly over the bases and to the edges.

Get everybody to choose toppings and build their pizzas. Finish with cheese, oregano and salt and pepper.

Place the pizzas under a preheated grill and cook for 5–10 minutes or until the toppings have cooked and the cheese has melted.

Heat the oil in a large, nonstick saucepan and lightly cook the onion and garlic until they are soft and lightly browned. Add the rice and cook for 1–2 minutes, stirring constantly, until the grains are golden.

Add the hot stock, tomatoes and broccoli and stir to combine. Cover the pan and simmer for about 25 minutes.

When the rice is nearly cooked add the sweetcorn and coriander and cook for a further 5 minutes or until the rice is just cooked.

Stir the risotto and season with salt and pepper or vegetable bouillon powder. Serve immediately.

COOK'S NOTES Ring the changes by replacing the frozen sweetcorn with baby corn and the broccoli with mangetout.

131 Cleopatra's rice

Preparation time:
15 minutes

Cooking time:
about 50 minutes

Serves: **4**

125 g (4 oz) green lentils, rinsed
1.2 litres (2 pints) vegetable stock
1 teaspoon ground cumin
1 teaspoon ground coriander
1 bay leaf
150 g (5 oz) basmati rice, rinsed
2 tablespoons sunflower oil
1 onion, finely chopped
1 garlic clove, crushed (optional)
4 teaspoons tahini paste (optional)
grated rind and juice of 1 lemon
2 courgettes, about 250 g (8 oz) in total,
  cut into sticks
1 teaspoon clear honey (optional)
150 g (5 oz) natural yogurt
1 tablespoon chopped mint (optional)
pitta bread, to serve

Put the lentils, 1 litre (1³/₄ pints) stock, the spices and bay leaf into a large saucepan. Bring to the boil, cover and simmer for 30–40 minutes or until tender, stirring occasionally.

Cook the rice separately in boiling water until tender, drain and rinse with hot water.

Heat 1 tablespoon oil in a nonstick frying pan, add the onion and garlic (if used) and fry until golden. Pour off and reserve the excess stock from the lentils. Add the fried onion, rice, tahini paste (if used), lemon rind and juice to the lentils. Cover and set aside until ready to serve.

Heat the remaining oil in a clean nonstick frying pan. Add the courgette sticks and stir-fry for 5 minutes or until lightly browned. Drizzle with honey (if used) and cook for 1 minute. Reheat the lentils, stirring, and moisten with the reserved stock if needed. Pile into serving bowls.

Flavour the yogurt with the mint, if liked, spoon on top of the lentils and surround with the courgette sticks. Serve with warm pitta bread.

132 Not fried rice

Preparation time:
10 minutes

Cooking time:
25 minutes

Serves: **2–3**

100 g (3¹/₂ oz) brown rice, rinsed
100 g (3¹/₂ oz) pearl barley, rinsed
600 ml (1 pint) vegetable stock
125 g (4 oz) can kidney beans, rinsed and
  drained
100 g (3¹/₂ oz) frozen peas
2 carrots, grated
handful of parsley, finely chopped
salt and pepper

Put the rice, barley and stock in a large pan and bring to the boil. Turn down the heat, cover and simmer for about 20 minutes or until the rice and barley are cooked.

Drain the rice and barley, return them to the pan and add the kidney beans. Cover the pan with a clean tea towel and the lid and set aside. The tea towel will absorb moisture and keep the grains separate.

Cook the peas in boiling water for 3–4 minutes. Drain and add to the rice mixture.

Stir the carrots and parsley into the rice mixture and season to taste. Serve immediately.

COOK'S NOTES For a bit of variety add sweetcorn, chopped courgettes and red peppers. If your child likes herbs and spices, add chopped coriander leaves and a pinch of ground cumin, while a few raisins, pine nuts and some grated orange rind will give the dish a North African flavour.

133 Carrot and rosemary risotto

134 Roast pumpkin and risotto

Preparation time:
15 minutes

Cooking time:
25–30 minutes

Serves: 2–3

2 tablespoons olive oil
1 onion, finely chopped
250 g (8 oz) carrots, diced
1–2 garlic cloves, crushed
few sprigs of rosemary, snipped
250 g (8 oz) arborio rice
1 litre (1³/₄ pints) vegetable stock
grated Parmesan cheese, to serve
(optional)

Heat the oil in a nonstick frying pan, add the onion and fry, stirring occasionally, for 5 minutes over medium heat or until pale golden.

Stir in the carrots, garlic, 1 tablespoon rosemary and the rice. Add one-quarter of the hot stock to the rice and simmer.

Keep a watch on the risotto as it cooks and top up with stock every 5 minutes or so until the rice is soft and the stock nearly all added. This should take about 20 minutes.

Spoon the risotto into warm dishes and top with the extra rosemary leaves and, if liked, grated Parmesan.

Preparation time:
20 minutes

Cooking time:
30–35 minutes

Oven temperature:
200°C (400°F), Gas Mark 6

Serves: 3–4

750 g (1¹/₂ lb) pumpkin, deseeded, peeled
and thickly sliced
250 g (8 oz) shallots, halved if large
3 tablespoons olive oil
¹/₂–1 red chilli, deseeded and finely diced
(optional)
2 rosemary stems, chopped, plus extra
sprigs to garnish
250 g (8 oz) arborio rice, rinsed
large pinch of saffron strands
1 litre (1³/₄ pints) vegetable stock
40 g (1¹/₂ oz) frozen peas or mixed
vegetables
salt and pepper

Scatter the pumpkin and two-thirds of the shallots in a roasting tin. Brush with 2 tablespoons oil. Sprinkle over the chilli (if used) and rosemary and season to taste. Roast in a preheated oven, 200°C (400°F), Gas Mark 6, for 30 minutes or until golden.

Meanwhile, finely chop the remaining shallots. Heat the remaining oil in a large, nonstick frying pan, add the shallots and fry until softened. Add the rice and cook, stirring, for 1 minute. Add the saffron and half the stock. Simmer, stirring, for 20 minutes or until creamy, topping up with extra stock as the rice cooks (you might not need all the stock).

Cook the frozen vegetables in boiling water for 3 minutes. Arrange the pumpkin and cooked vegetables on warm serving plates, add the risotto and serve garnished with rosemary.

COOK'S NOTES This risotto is also delicious made with sweet potato in place of the carrot.

135 Mixed vegetable risotto

Preparation time:
15 minutes

Cooking time:
about 25 minutes

Serves: **4**

2 tablespoons olive oil
1 garlic clove, crushed
300 g (10 oz) arborio rice, rinsed
1 litre (1³/₄ pints) vegetable stock
**250 g (8 oz) broccoli, cut in small florets
    and stalks sliced**
125 g (4 oz) frozen peas
150 g (5 oz) baby spinach
**25 g (1 oz) Parmesan cheese, grated, plus
    shavings to garnish**
salt and pepper

Heat the oil in a large, heavy-based saucepan, add the garlic and rice and fry for 1 minute. Pour in the stock and bring to the boil. Reduce the heat and simmer gently for 15–20 minutes, stirring frequently, until the mixture is creamy and the rice is just tender.

Add the broccoli and peas to the risotto and cook for a further 5 minutes, stirring frequently to prevent the rice from sticking to the base of the pan. Add a little more water if the risotto becomes dry.

Stir in the spinach and cook for 1–2 minutes or until the leaves have wilted. Stir in the grated Parmesan and season to taste. Spoon on to warm serving plates and garnish with Parmesan shavings.

COOK'S NOTES A risotto should have a moist, creamy consistency. This recipe is unusual in adding all the stock at once rather than small amounts as the rice absorbs. Stir in a little hot water or stock if the rice starts to dry out.

136 Marinated tofu and stir-fried vegetables

Preparation time:
**20 minutes, plus
marinating**

Cooking time:
about 10 minutes

Serves: **3–4**

285 g (9¹/₂ oz) chilled tofu, drained
4 teaspoons tomato ketchup
4 teaspoons soy sauce
6 teaspoons sunflower oil
**2.5 cm (1 inch) fresh root ginger, peeled
    and finely chopped**
1 garlic clove, crushed
2 sheets dried egg noodles
1 red pepper, halved, cored and deseeded
1 large courgette, about 200 g (7 oz)
75 g (3 oz) mangetout, halved lengthways
**3 spring onions, trimmed and thickly
    sliced, plus extra, shredded, to serve**

Cut the tofu into 3–4 pieces and score criss-cross lines on both sides. Mix together the ketchup, soy sauce, 3 teaspoons oil, the ginger and garlic in a large, shallow dish, add the tofu and to coat in the marinade. Set aside for 30 minutes.

Reserve the marinade and transfer the tofu to a foil-lined grill pan and grill for 5 minutes until browned, turning once.

Meanwhile, cook the noodles in boiling water according to the instructions on the packet.

Cut the pepper and courgette into thin strips. Heat the remaining oil in a large, nonstick frying pan or wok and add the pepper, courgette, mangetout and sliced spring onions and stir-fry over a high heat for about 3 minutes. Drain the noodles and add to the stir-fry. Cook, stirring, for a further 30 seconds.

Stir the reserved marinade into the stir-fry. Spoon the vegetables on to warm plates and top with the tofu. Serve garnished with shredded spring onion.

137 Cauliflower and lentil dhal

138 Vegetable quartet with parsnip mash

Preparation time:
15 minutes

Cooking time:
40 minutes

Serves: **3–4**

175 g (6 oz) red lentils, rinsed
1 teaspoon turmeric
1 teaspoon finely ground cumin seeds
375 g (12 oz) cauliflower, cut into florets
400 g (13 oz) potatoes, diced
200 g (7 oz) basmati rice, rinsed
4 teaspoons sunflower oil
1 onion, thinly sliced
2 garlic cloves, sliced
1 teaspoon black mustard seeds
¹/₂ teaspoon cumin seeds, roughly
  crushed
3 tomatoes, about 175 g (6 oz), skinned,
  deseeded and chopped
3 tablespoons chopped fresh coriander
  (optional), plus extra sprigs to garnish
chilli sauce, to taste
salt and pepper
naan bread or chapatis, to serve

Put the lentils in a saucepan with 900 ml (1¹/₂ pints) water, the turmeric and cumin. Bring to the boil, cover and simmer for 20 minutes or until almost tender. Add the cauliflower and potatoes to the pan, stir and top up with extra water if needed. Cover and simmer gently for 15 minutes.

Meanwhile, bring 450 ml (³/₄ pint) water to the boil in a separate pan. Add the rice, cover and simmer for 10 minutes. Turn off the heat and leave to stand, covered, for 5 minutes.

Heat the oil in a nonstick frying pan and add the onion, garlic, mustard and cumin seeds and fry for 5 minutes or until golden. Add the tomato and coriander (if used) to the pan. Season with salt and pepper and add chilli sauce to taste.

Spoon the rice and dhal on to warm plates and top with the spiced onion and tomato mixture. Garnish with coriander and serve with warm naan bread or chapatis.

Preparation time:
15 minutes

Cooking time:
about 20 minutes

Serves: **2–3**

750 g (1¹/₂ lb) parsnips, halved, cored and
  cut into chunks
3 baby leeks, about 75 g (3 oz), well
  washed and thickly sliced
100 g (3¹/₂ oz) green beans, halved
150 g (5 oz) frozen baby broad beans
125 g (4 oz) broccoli, cut into florets
4 teaspoons olive oil
2 tablespoons pumpkin seeds
2 tablespoons sesame seeds
25 g (1 oz) butter
4 tablespoons fromage frais
3 tablespoons full-fat milk
2 teaspoons sun-dried tomato paste
juice of ¹/₂ lemon
salt and pepper (optional)

Cook the parsnips in boiling water in the base of a steamer for 10 minutes. Put the other vegetables in the top of the steamer, cover and cook for 5 minutes or until just tender.

Meanwhile, heat 1 teaspoon oil in a nonstick frying pan, add the pumpkin and sesame seeds and fry until golden.

Drain the parsnips and mash smoothly. Add the butter, fromage frais and milk to the parsnip mash and mix well.

Toss the green vegetables with the tomato paste, remaining olive oil and lemon juice and season with salt and pepper to taste. Spoon on to warm plates, add the parsnip mash and serve sprinkled with the toasted seeds.

COOK'S NOTES A medley of green vegetables tossed in a lemon and tomato dressing and served with a smooth, creamy parsnip mash makes a quick and easy midweek supper.

139 Smoky joes

140 Eggs florentine

Preparation time:
15 minutes

Cooking time:
40 minutes

Serves: **3–4**

2 aubergines, about 500 g (1 lb) in total
2 tablespoons olive oil
2 courgettes, about 300 g (10 oz) in total,
cut into sticks
1 onion, finely chopped
1 garlic clove, crushed
6 small flour tortillas
200 g (7 oz) can red kidney beans,
drained
1 teaspoon hot chilli sauce, or to taste
3 tablespoons chopped fresh coriander
1 small lettuce, shredded
1 tablespoon grated mild Cheddar cheese
(optional)
salt and pepper

TO GARNISH:
lime wedges
coriander sprigs

Pierce the stalk end of each aubergine with a fork. Place on the grill rack and grill for 30 minutes, turning several times, until the skin is blackened and charred all over. Cool slightly, then peel off the skin. Chop the flesh and set aside.

Heat 1 tablespoon oil in a nonstick frying pan, add the courgette sticks and fry for 5 minutes or until tender. Remove with a slotted spoon. Heat the remaining oil in the pan, add the onion and garlic, and fry for 5 minutes or until softened. Add the aubergine and heat through.

Warm the tortillas according to the instructions on the packet.

Add the kidney beans to the aubergine mixture with the chilli sauce and chopped coriander. Heat through and add salt and pepper to taste.

Spoon the lettuce, aubergine and courgette on to the tortillas, scatter the cheese (if used) and roll up. Serve with lime wedges and coriander.

Preparation time:
15 minutes

Cooking time:
25–30 minutes

Oven temperature:
190°C (375°F), Gas Mark 5

Serves: **3**

500 g (1 lb) potatoes, thinly sliced
375 g (12 oz) spinach, stems removed
25 g (1 oz) butter, plus extra for greasing
pinch of grated nutmeg
3 eggs
25 g (1 oz) plain flour
325 ml (11 fl oz) full-fat milk
125 g (4 oz) medium Cheddar cheese,
grated
1 teaspoon Dijon mustard (optional)
2 tablespoons breadcrumbs
salt and pepper
thyme sprigs, to garnish (optional)

Cook the potatoes in the base of a steamer for 5 minutes or until just tender, steaming the spinach above for 3 minutes or until just wilted. Drain the potatoes, rinse with cold water and drain again.

Spoon the potatoes into a buttered, 1.5 litre (2¹/₂ pint) ovenproof dish. Top with the spinach and season with salt, pepper and nutmeg.

Poach the eggs by sliding them into simmering water. Cook for 2–3 minutes or until the egg whites are set but the yolks are still soft. Carefully lift them out of the pan with a slotted spoon, drain well and place them on top of the spinach.

Melt the butter in a saucepan, stir in the flour and cook for 1 minute, then gradually whisk in the milk. Bring to the boil, whisking until thick and smooth. Stir in two-thirds of the cheese, flavour with the mustard (if used) and season to taste. Pour the sauce over the eggs and sprinkle with the remaining cheese and the breadcrumbs. Bake in a preheated oven, 190°C (375°F), Gas Mark 5, for 15 minutes or until the cheese is bubbling and golden. Garnish with thyme sprigs, if liked.

COOK'S NOTES Use 250 g (8 oz) frozen spinach instead of fresh leaves. Thaw and squeeze out excess moisture, then arrange on top of the potatoes. There is no need to precook.

141 Roasted vegetables and cheese

Preparation time: **15 minutes**	**2 sweet potatoes, about 500 g (1 lb) in total, scrubbed and thinly sliced** **2 small red onions, cut into wedges**

Cooking time:
35 minutes
	**2 red peppers, cored, deseeded and cut
	    into wedges**
	**1 yellow pepper, cored, deseeded and
	    cut into wedges**

Oven temperature: **200°C (400°F), Gas Mark 6**	**3 courgettes, cut into chunks** **5 tablespoons olive oil** **1 garlic clove, crushed**
Serves: **4**	**finely grated rind and juice of 1 lemon** **2 tablespoons clear honey** **200 g (7 oz) haloumi or feta cheese, drained and diced** **salt and pepper**

TO SERVE:
lemon wedges (optional)
green salad
ciabatta or wholegrain bread

Put the sweet potatoes in a large roasting tin with the onions, peppers and courgettes. Add 2 tablespoons oil and toss the ingredients together. Roast the vegetables in a preheated oven, 200°C (400°F), Gas Mark 6, for about 30 minutes or until they are golden, tossing them once or twice during roasting.

Meanwhile, mix together the remaining oil with the garlic, lemon rind and juice, honey and salt and pepper.

Scatter the cheese over the vegetables and cook for a further 5 minutes. Transfer to warm serving plates, spoon on the dressing, and serve with lemon wedges, if liked, and a green salad and warm ciabatta or crusty, grainy bread.

COOK'S NOTES Roasted vegetables are delicious on their own but are even better tossed with tangy cheese and a sweet honey dressing.

142 Stuffed vegetables with couscous

Preparation time: **15 minutes**	**2 beefsteak tomatoes** **2 red, orange or yellow peppers, halved, cored and deseeded**
Cooking time: **30 minutes**	**2 tablespoons olive oil** **175 g (6 oz) couscous** **300 ml (1/2 pint) boiling water**

Oven temperature:
200°C (400°F), Gas Mark 6
	**1/2 bunch of spring onions, trimmed and
	    sliced**
	**small handful of basil leaves, torn into
	    pieces**

Serves: **4**	**125 g (4 oz) mozzarella cheese, drained
	    and chopped**
	25 g (1 oz) Parmesan cheese, grated
	**400 g (13 oz) can chickpeas, rinsed and
	    drained**
	salt and pepper

Halve the tomatoes horizontally and scoop out the pulp and seeds. Put the tomatoes and peppers, cut side up, in a large, shallow, ovenproof dish and drizzle with the oil and a little salt and pepper. Bake in a preheated oven, 200°C (400°F), Gas Mark 6, for 20 minutes or until they have softened.

Meanwhile, put the couscous in a bowl, pour on the measured boiling water and leave to stand for 10 minutes or until the water is absorbed. Fluff up the couscous with a fork and stir in the spring onions, basil, mozzarella, Parmesan, chickpeas and add salt and pepper to taste.

Spoon the couscous mixture into the baked vegetables and return the dish to the oven for a further 8–10 minutes or until the vegetables have heated through and the mozzarella has melted. Serve warm, with a leafy salad and warm bread.

COOK'S NOTES Peppers and large tomatoes make perfect containers for savoury stuffings and roast to a sweet tenderness. Chickpeas add texture and flavour but they can be left out, or replaced with a sprinkling of toasted pine nuts if preferred.

143 Vegetable chilli with salsa

144 Quick vegetable korma

Preparation time:
20 minutes

Cooking time:
30 minutes

Serves: **4**

3 tablespoons oil
2 red onions, chopped
2 celery sticks, sliced
3 carrots, sliced
2 teaspoons dark muscovado sugar
2 red peppers, cored, deseeded and roughly chopped
2 garlic cloves, crushed
400 g (13 oz) can chopped tomatoes
400 g (13 oz) can red kidney beans or borlotti beans, rinsed and drained
1 tablespoon mild chilli seasoning
300 ml (1/2 pint) vegetable stock
salt and pepper
rice, to serve

AVOCADO SALSA:
1 large ripe avocado, stoned and peeled
7.5 cm (3 inch) cucumber, diced
1 tablespoon lemon juice
1 teaspoon caster sugar
2 tablespoons roughly chopped fresh coriander

Preparation time:
15 minutes

Cooking time:
35 minutes

Serves: **4**

3 tablespoons vegetable oil
25 g (1 oz) flaked almonds
2 onions, sliced
10 cardamom pods (optional)
2.5 cm (1 inch) fresh root ginger, peeled and grated (optional)
1 teaspoon ground turmeric
2 garlic cloves, sliced
2 teaspoons medium curry paste
4 carrots, thinly sliced
1 cauliflower, cut into florets
450 ml (3/4 pint) vegetable stock
2 courgettes, sliced
125 g (4 oz) frozen peas
200 ml (7 fl oz) coconut milk
50 g (2 oz) ground almonds
3 tablespoons double cream
salt and pepper

TO SERVE:
basmati rice or naan bread
mango chutney

Heat the oil in a large, heavy-based saucepan. Add the onions, celery, carrots and sugar and fry gently for 6–8 minutes or until the vegetables are deep golden. Add the peppers and garlic and fry for 2 minutes.

Stir in the tomatoes, beans, chilli seasoning and stock and bring to the boil and simmer, uncovered, for 20 minutes or until the vegetables are tender and the sauce has thickened. Check the seasoning.

Meanwhile, make the salsa. Finely chop the avocado flesh and place it in a bowl with the cucumber, lemon juice, sugar and coriander. Toss to mix and season with salt and pepper to taste.

Serve the vegetable chilli with rice and the avocado salsa.

Heat the oil in a large, heavy-based saucepan. Add the flaked almonds and fry gently for 1–2 minutes or until toasted. Remove with a slotted spoon and set aside.

Add the onions, cardamom pods and ginger (if used), turmeric, garlic and curry paste to the pan. Fry gently for 5 minutes. Add the carrots and cauliflower and fry for a further 5 minutes or until coloured. Add the stock and bring to the boil. Cover the pan and simmer gently for 20 minutes or until the vegetables are tender.

Add the courgettes, peas, coconut milk and ground almonds. Bring back to a simmer and cook gently, uncovered, for 3 minutes. Stir in the cream and add salt and pepper to taste. Scatter over the flaked almonds and serve with basmati rice or naan and mango chutney.

145 Savoury clafoutis

Preparation time:
10 minutes

Cooking time:
25 minutes

Oven temperature:
200°C (400°F), Gas Mark 6

Serves: **4**

butter, for greasing
500 g (1 lb) tomatoes (preferably vine), quartered
250 g (8 oz) button mushrooms, halved if large
75 g (3 oz) pepperoni or salami, thinly sliced (optional)
6 eggs
25 g (1 oz) plain white flour
50 g (2 oz) watercress, tough stalks removed
200 ml (7 fl oz) semi-skimmed milk
50 g (2 oz) Gruyère cheese, grated
salt and pepper

TO SERVE:
green salad
wholegrain bread or potatoes

Lightly butter 4 individual pie dishes or gratin dishes. Scatter the tomatoes and mushrooms into the dishes. If you are cooking for non-vegetarians, add the pepperoni or salami.

Put the eggs, flour, watercress, milk and a little salt and pepper into a food processor or blender and process until they are evenly blended and the watercress is finely chopped. Pour into the dishes and sprinkle with the cheese.

Bake in a preheated oven, 200°C (400°F), Gas Mark 6, for about 25 minutes or until pale golden and lightly set. Serve immediately with a leafy salad and grainy bread or potatoes.

COOK'S NOTES If you can get them use vine tomatoes in this recipe. It's worth investing in some individual ovenproof dishes for vegetarian meals so they can be cooked separately from any meaty dished.

146 Wholewheat salad and chilli tomatoes

Preparation time:
15 minutes

Cooking time:
20 minutes

Serves:
1 vegetarian and 3 meat-eaters

250 g (8 oz) precooked wholewheat grains
6 lamb cutlets
750 g (1½ lb) vine tomatoes
3 tablespoons olive oil
3 tablespoons balsamic vinegar
1 mild red chilli, cored, deseeded and thinly sliced
4 tablespoons snipped chives or 2 spring onions, trimmed and finely chopped
50 g (2 oz) pine nuts
50 g (2 oz) rocket or baby spinach
1 small red onion, cut into rings
50 g (2 oz) feta, Cheddar or Cheshire cheese, crumbled
salt and pepper

Cook the wholewheat in lightly salted, boiling water for 20 minutes or until tender.

Meanwhile, cut any excess fat from the lamb and season it lightly on both sides with salt and pepper. When the wholewheat is almost cooked, put the lamb on a grill rack under a preheated high grill and cook for 5 minutes on each side.

Meanwhile, quarter the tomatoes. Scoop the seeds and pulp into a sieve over a large bowl and press with the back of a spoon to extract the juice. Add the tomato quarters and their juice to the bowl with the oil, vinegar and chilli. Season to taste.

Drain the wholewheat and return it to the pan. Add the chives or spring onions, pine nuts, rocket or spinach, and a little more salt and pepper if needed. Spoon on to warm serving plates and top with the tomato mixture and the red onion rings. Add the grilled cutlets to 3 servings and sprinkle the crumbled cheese over the vegetarian portion.

Preparation time:
10 minutes

Cooking time:
25 minutes

Serves: **4**

3 tablespoons olive oil
1 large onion, chopped
2 celery sticks, sliced
2 garlic cloves, crushed
400 g (13 oz) can chopped tomatoes
1 teaspoon ground cumin
1 teaspoon ground coriander
1 tablespoon paprika
400 g (13 oz) can mixed beans, cannellini or haricot beans, rinsed and drained
400 g (13 oz) can chickpeas, rinsed and drained
50 g (2 oz) dried apricots, sliced
300 ml (1/2 pint) chicken or vegetable stock
250 g (8 oz) couscous
300 ml (1/2 pint) boiling water
salt and pepper
celery leaves (if available) or flat leaf parsley, to garnish

Preparation time:
10 minutes

Cooking time:
30–35 minutes

Serves: **4**

2 tablespoons vegetable oil
1 large onion, chopped
2 celery sticks, sliced
500 g (1 lb) carrots, sliced
1 garlic clove, crushed
150 g (5 oz) split red lentils, rinsed
1.4 litres (2 1/4 pints) vegetable stock
salt and pepper

SPICED BUTTER (OPTIONAL):
40 g (1 1/2 oz) lightly salted butter, softened
2 spring onions, trimmed and finely chopped
1/4 teaspoon dried chilli flakes
1 teaspoon cumin seeds, lightly crushed
finely grated rind of 1 lemon
small handful of fresh coriander, chopped
several mint sprigs, chopped

Heat the oil in a large, heavy-based saucepan, add the onion, celery and garlic and fry gently for 5 minutes. Stir in the tomatoes, spices, beans, chickpeas, dried apricots and stock and bring to the boil. Simmer gently, uncovered, for about 20 minutes or until the vegetables are tender and the sauce is pulpy.

Meanwhile, put the couscous into a bowl with a little salt and pepper. Add the measured boiling water and cover. Leave in a warm place for 5–10 minutes or until the water has been absorbed. Fluff up lightly with a fork.

Spoon the couscous on to warm serving plates and top with the sauce. Serve garnished with celery leaves or flat leaf parsley.

COOK'S NOTES The selection of vegetables, beans and spices create an appetizing dish that's equally suitable for lunch or supper.

Make the spiced butter (if used). Put all the ingredients in a bowl and beat them together until combined. Transfer to a small serving dish, cover and chill until needed.

Heat the oil in a large, heavy-based saucepan. Add the onion and celery and cook gently for 5 minutes or until softened. Add the carrots and garlic and fry for 3 minutes.

Add the lentils and stock and bring just to the boil, cover and cook gently for 20–25 minutes or until the vegetables are soft and the soup is pulpy. Season to taste.

Spoon the soup into warm bowls. Serve the spiced butter (if used) separately so that diners can stir in as much as they like.

6 Desserts

149 Vanilla and banana pancakes

150 Lacy apricot pancakes

Preparation time: 20 minutes	**2 bananas** **1 teaspoon vanilla extract** **125 g (4 oz) self-raising flour**
Cooking time: 20–25 minutes	**1 teaspoon baking powder** **1 tablespoon caster sugar** **1 egg**
Makes: 12 pancakes	**125 ml (4 fl oz) milk** **15 g (½ oz) unsalted butter, melted** **oil, for frying**

FUDGE SAUCE:
75 g (3 oz) unsalted butter, diced
150 g (5 oz) light muscovado sugar
175 g (6 oz) can evaporated milk

Preparation time: 15 minutes	**4 scoops vanilla ice cream** **sifted icing sugar, to decorate**
Cooking time: about 15 minutes	PANCAKES: **50 g (2 oz) plain flour** **1 egg**
Serves: **4**	**125 ml (4 fl oz) full-fat milk** **1 teaspoon sunflower oil, plus extra for** **frying**

FILLING:
375 g (12 oz) apricots, stoned and diced
1 dessert apple, quartered, cored, peeled
and diced
4 tablespoons apple juice

Mash the bananas with the vanilla extract to make a purée. Sift the flour and baking powder into a bowl and stir in the sugar. Beat the egg with the milk and melted butter and beat into the dry ingredients until smooth. Stir in the banana purée.

Heat a little oil in a large, nonstick frying pan. Using a large metal spoon, drop in spoonfuls of the batter, spacing them well apart in the pan. Cook for about 3 minutes or until bubbles appear on the surface and the undersides are golden. Turn the pancakes and cook for an additional 1–2 minutes. Keep warm while you cook the remainder.

Make the sauce. Put the butter in a small, heavy-based saucepan with the sugar. Heat gently, stirring, until the butter has melted and the sugar has dissolved. Bring to boil and boil for 2 minutes.

Remove the pan from the heat and pour in the evaporated milk. Stir gently to combine. Return the pan to the heat, bring to the boil and cook for 1 minute until smooth and glossy. Serve hot with the pancakes.

Make the filling by putting the apricots, apple and apple juice in a small saucepan, cover and simmer for 5 minutes. Set aside to cool slightly.

Make the pancakes. Put the flour in a bowl, add the egg and gradually whisk in the milk until smooth and frothy. Whisk in the oil. Heat a little oil in a small frying pan until it is very hot; pour off any excess oil. Drizzle pancake batter over the base of the pan to give a lacy effect. Cook for 2–3 minutes or until golden, then loosen the pancake, toss and cook until the other side is golden.

Slide the pancake on to a warm plate and keep hot. Continue making pancakes in this way until all the batter is used, stacking the cooked pancakes between sheets of greaseproof paper.

Put a pancake on each serving plate and place a spoonful of the warm apricot compote and a scoop of ice cream on one side. Fold the pancake over the filling and dust lightly with icing sugar.

COOK'S NOTE Use dried or canned apricots when fresh ones are out of season. Alternatively, use ripe plums.

151 Lemon meringue pie

152 Key lime pie

Preparation time:
35 minutes, plus chilling

Cooking time:
50 minutes

Oven temperature:
200°C (400°F), Gas Mark 6

Serves: 6

175 g (6 oz) sweet shortcrust pastry
  (thawed if frozen)
25 g (1 oz) cornflour
100 g (3¹/₂ oz) caster sugar
150 ml (¹/₄ pint) water
grated rind of 2 lemons
juice of 1 lemon
25 g (1 oz) unsalted butter
2 egg yolks

MERINGUE:
3 egg whites
175 g (6 oz) caster sugar

Roll out the pastry on a lightly floured surface and line a 20 cm (8 inch) tart tin. Chill for 30 minutes, then bake blind in a preheated oven for 15 minutes. Remove the paper and beans or foil and return to the oven for a further 5 minutes.

Mix the cornflour and caster sugar in a saucepan. Stir in the water, lemon rind and juice until well blended. Bring to the boil, stirring until the sauce is thickened and smooth. Take it off the heat and stir in the butter. Leave to cool slightly.

Beat the egg yolks in a bowl. Whisk in 2 tablespoons of the sauce and return this mixture to the pan. Cook gently until it has thickened further and pour into the pastry case. Return to the oven for 15 minutes or until the filling has set.

Whisk the egg whites until stiff and dry. Whisk in 1 tablespoon of sugar, then fold in the rest. Spread the mixture so that it completely covers the filling. Return to the oven for 10 minutes or until the meringue is golden. Serve warm or cold.

COOK'S NOTE For best results whisk the egg whites in a clean, dry and grease-free bowl. Some cooks like to add a pinch of salt or a few drops of lemon juice to help the foam keep its shape.

Preparation time:
30 minutes, plus chilling

Cooking time:
15–20 minutes

Oven temperature:
160°C (325°F), Gas Mark 3

Serves: 8

PIE CRUST:
175 g (6 oz) digestive biscuit crumbs
2 tablespoons caster sugar
75 g (3 oz) unsalted butter, melted

FILLING:
3 eggs, separated
425 g (14 oz) can sweetened condensed
  milk
125 ml (4 fl oz) lime juice
1 tablespoon lemon juice
2 teaspoons grated lime rind
2 tablespoons caster sugar

TOPPING:
250 ml (8 fl oz) double cream
1 tablespoon icing sugar
few drops of vanilla extract
slices of lime, to decorate

Mix together the crust ingredients and press over the bottom and up the sides of a 23 cm (9 inch) springform tin. Chill.

Lightly beat the egg yolks until creamy. Add the condensed milk, lime and lemon juices and lime rind and beat until well mixed and slightly thickened. In another bowl beat the egg whites until frothy. Add the sugar and continue beating until the meringue holds soft peaks. Fold gently but thoroughly into the lime mixture.

Spoon the filling into the crumb crust and smooth the top. Bake in a preheated oven, 160°C (325°F), Gas Mark 3, for 15–20 minutes or until the filling is just firm and lightly browned on top. When cool refrigerate for at least 3 hours, until the pie is well chilled.

Whip the cream until it begins to thicken, add the sugar and vanilla extract and whip until thick but not stiff. Spread over the top of the pie. Remove the side of the tin and serve decorated with lime slices.

153 Blueberry pie

154 Warm berry brûlée

Preparation time:
25 minutes, plus chilling

Cooking time:
30–35 minutes

Oven temperature:
190°C (375°F), Gas Mark 5

Serves: **6**

**375 g (12 oz) sweet shortcrust pastry
(thawed if frozen)
250 g (8 oz) fresh or frozen blueberries
(thawed if frozen)
25 g (1 oz) sugar
milk, to glaze
50 g (2 oz) flaked almonds, to decorate
cream or crème fraîche, to serve**

Roll out about two-thirds of the pastry on a lightly floured surface and line a 23 cm (9 inch) tart tin. Chill for 30 minutes. Spread the blueberries evenly over the pastry case and sprinkle with the sugar.

Roll out the remaining pastry and cut into thin strips. Brush the rim of the tart with water and arrange the pastry strips in a lattice pattern over the top. Brush the pastry with a little milk and sprinkle the flaked almonds over the surface.

Bake in a preheated oven, 190°C (375°F), Gas Mark 5, for 30–35 minutes or until the pastry is golden and the blueberries are tender. Serve warm or cold with cream or crème fraîche.

Preparation time:
20 minutes, plus cooling

Cooking time:
30–35 minutes

Oven temperature:
180°C (350°F), Gas Mark 4

Serves: **6**

**250 g (8 oz) mixed red berries
8 egg yolks
75 g (3 oz) caster sugar
1 teaspoon vanilla extract
250 ml (8 fl oz) crème fraîche
250 ml (8 fl oz) double cream
50 g (2 oz) caster sugar, to finish
selection of fresh berries dusted with
icing sugar, to serve**

Arrange 6 ovenproof ramekins in a roasting tin and divide the berries among them. Lightly mix together the egg yolks, sugar, vanilla extract and crème fraîche. Pour the double cream into a saucepan and bring almost to the boil. Gradually stir it into the yolk mixture.

Strain the mixture into the ramekins and mix the fruits into the cream with a fork. Pour warm water into the roasting tin so that it comes halfway up the side of the dishes and bake in a preheated oven, 180°C (350°F), Gas Mark 4, for 25–30 minutes or until the custards are set with a slight softness at the centre.

Remove the dishes from the tin and leave to cool at room temperature for about 1 hour. Sprinkle the tops with the sugar and caramelize with a blowtorch. Serve within 30 minutes, decorated with extra berries dusted with icing sugar.

COOK'S NOTE Fresh blueberries have a fairly short season, but frozen berries are available and can be used equally successfully in this pie. The flavour of the fruit is intensified by cooking.

155 Triple chocolate brûlée

156 Sticky toffee puddings

Preparation time:
**30 minutes, plus freezing
and chilling**

Cooking time:
5 minutes

Serves: **6**

8 egg yolks
50 g (2 oz) caster sugar
600 ml (1 pint) double cream
**125 g (4 oz) plain dark chocolate, finely
    chopped**
**125 g (4 oz) white chocolate, finely
    chopped**
**125 g (4 oz) milk chocolate, finely
    chopped**
50 g (2 oz) caster sugar, to finish
**plain dark, white and milk chocolate
    curls, to decorate (optional)**

Mix together the egg yolks and sugar in a bowl. Pour the cream into a saucepan and bring almost to the boil. Gradually beat the cream into the yolk mixture. Strain the custard into a measuring jug and divide it equally among 3 bowls. Stir a different chocolate into each bowl of hot custard. Stir until melted.

Divide the plain dark chocolate custard among 6 ramekins. When cool, transfer the dishes to the freezer for 10 minutes to chill and set.

Remove the ramekins from the freezer, stir the white chocolate custard and spoon it over the dark layer. Return to the freezer for 10 minutes.

Remove the dishes from the freezer, stir the milk chocolate custard and spoon it into the dishes. Chill the custards for 3–4 hours until set.

About 25 minutes before serving sprinkle the tops of the dishes with the remaining sugar and caramelize with a blowtorch. Leave the custards at room temperature until ready to serve and decorate with chocolate curls, if liked.

Preparation time:
20 minutes

Cooking time:
45–50 minutes

Oven temperature:
180°C (350°F), Gas Mark 4

Serves: **8**

125 g (4 oz) pitted dried dates, chopped
125 g (4 oz) unsalted butter, softened
150 g (4 oz) caster sugar
2 teaspoons vanilla bean paste
3 eggs
150 g (5 oz) self-raising flour
1 teaspoon baking powder
cream or ice cream, to serve

SAUCE:
300 ml (½ pint) double cream
175 g (6 oz) light brown sugar
65 g (2½ oz) unsalted butter

Put the dates in a small saucepan with 125 ml (4 fl oz) water and bring to the boil. Simmer gently for 5 minutes or until the dates are soft and pulpy. Blend to a purée in a food processor and leave to cool.

Meanwhile, make the sauce. Put half the cream in a small, heavy-based saucepan with the sugar and butter and heat until the sugar dissolves. Bring to the boil and allow the sauce to bubble for about 5 minutes or until it turns rich, dark caramel in colour. Stir in the remaining cream and reserve.

Lightly grease 8 metal pudding moulds, each holding 125 ml (4 fl oz), and line the bases with circles of greaseproof paper. Put the unsalted butter, caster sugar, vanilla bean paste, eggs, flour and baking powder in a bowl and mix together until pale and creamy. Stir the date purée into the mixture and divide it among the pudding moulds. Level the tops and place the moulds in a roasting tin. Pour boiling water to a depth of about 2 cm (³/₄ inch) into the tin, cover with foil and bake the puddings in a preheated oven, 180°C (350°F), Gas Mark 4, for 35–40 minutes or until they are risen and feel firm to the touch.

Leave the puddings in the moulds while you reheat the sauce, then loosen the edges of the moulds and invert the puddings on to serving plates. Cover with the sauce and serve with cream or ice cream.

157 Fruit kebabs

158 Fruit salad

Preparation time: **15 minutes**	**1 mango, peeled and stoned** **250 g (8 oz) fresh pineapple** **2 large bananas**
Makes: **16–20 skewers**	**250 g (8 oz) strawberries, hulled** **125 g (4 oz) green seedless grapes** **125 g (4 oz) black seedless grapes**

TO SERVE:
lime juice
clear honey (optional)

Chop the mango, pineapple and bananas into chunks about 2.5 cm (1 inch) thick. Cut large strawberries in half.

Thread a piece of each fruit on to each bamboo skewer and arrange on a serving platter. To serve, squeeze a little lime juice over the skewers and drizzle with honey (if used).

Preparation time: **15 minutes**	**1 galia or ogen melon, skinned and** **deseeded** **1 small pineapple**
Serves: **4**	**2 kiwifruit, peeled** **125 g (4 oz) green seedless grapes** **finely grated rind and juice of 2 limes** **2 tablespoons clear honey**

Cut the melon flesh into cubes and put them into a serving bowl.

Cut the top and skin from the pineapple and remove the core. Cut the flesh into pieces and add to the melon.

Cut the flesh of the kiwifruit in dice. Halve the grapes and add them, with the kiwifruit, to the melon.

Add the lime rind and juice to the fruit mixture. Spoon the honey over, mix all the fruits together and serve.

COOK'S NOTE These fruit kebabs make a delicious and nutritious dessert on their own but are also great served with fruit yogurt for dipping.

Preparation time:	**1 large mango, halved and pitted**
10 minutes	**1 papaya, skinned and deseeded**
	1 small pineapple
Cooking time:	**2 kiwifruit, peeled and quartered**
5 minutes	**25 g (1 oz) unsalted butter, melted**
	1 piece preserved stem ginger, plus
Serves: **4**	**2 tablespoons syrup from the jar**
	2 passion fruit (optional)

Cut the flesh of the mango and papaya into pieces. Cut the top and skin from the pineapple and remove the core. Cut the flesh into pieces.

Line a grill pan with foil, bringing the foil up over the sides of the pan to contain the juices. Arrange all the fruits in the pan in a single layer. Brush with butter and spoon over the ginger syrup.

Thinly slice the stem ginger and cut each slice into thin slivers. Scatter over the fruits and grill for about 5 minutes or until the fruits are beginning to colour. Transfer to serving bowls, adding any juices from the pan.

Halve the passion fruit (if used), scoop out the pulp and spoon over the warm fruit salad to serve.

Preparation time:	CHOCOLATE SAUCE:
15 minutes	**50 g (2 oz) milk chocolate, chopped**
	75 g (3 oz) plain dark chocolate, chopped
Cooking time:	**75 ml (3 fl oz) full-fat milk**
10 minutes	**2 teaspoons golden syrup**
Serves: **4**	DUNKERS:
	1 red-skinned apple, cored
	2 peaches, stoned
	1 kiwifruit, peeled
	250 g (8 oz) strawberries
	1 banana, peeled and thickly sliced

Put the chocolate in a small saucepan with the milk and golden syrup. Heat gently, stirring occasionally, until melted and smooth. Pour the chocolate sauce into 4 small dishes and set each one on a larger individual serving plate.

Cut the apple, peaches and kiwifruit into chunks. Halve or quarter the strawberries, depending on size.

Arrange all the fruit on the serving plates. Provide small forks so that children can dunk the fruits into the warm sauce before eating.

COOK'S NOTE It can be difficult to judge if a mango is ripe because colour is not necessarily a good indication. Avoid blotchy fruits that have black spots, which indicate over-ripeness. A ripe fruit should give gently when pressed and have a slight fragrance.

161 Pink blush jellies

Preparation time:
15 minutes, plus chilling

Cooking time:
10 minutes

Serves: **4**

125 g (4 oz) redcurrants, stalks removed
250 ml (8 fl oz) water
100 g (3¹/₂ oz) strawberries
75 g (3 oz) seedless red grapes, halved
300 ml (¹/₂ pint) apple juice
1 sachet or 3 teaspoons powdered gelatine
50 g (2 oz) caster sugar
redcurrant sprigs, to decorate (optional)

Rinse the redcurrants and put them in a saucepan with the measured water. Bring to the boil and simmer for 5 minutes. Press through a sieve to remove skins.

Divide the strawberries and grapes among 4 individual jelly moulds, each holding 150 ml (¹/₄ pint).

Pour the apple juice into a saucepan, sprinkle over the gelatine and stir until dissolved, then add the redcurrant juice and sugar. Bring to the boil, stirring, until thickened, then pour straight into the jelly moulds. Allow to cool, then refrigerate for 2–3 hours until set.

To turn out the jellies briefly dip each mould into a bowl of hot water. Loosen the edges with your fingertips and invert the mould on to a serving plate. Holding the mould and plate together, jerk the mould to release the jelly, then remove. Serve the jellies topped with redcurrant sprigs, if liked.

162 Strawberry sundae jellies

Preparation time:
15 minutes, plus chilling

Serves: **4**

135 g (4¹/₂ oz) strawberry jelly tablet
300 ml (¹/₂ pint) water
250 g (8 oz) fresh strawberries, hulled, plus extra to decorate
200 g (7 oz) fromage frais
2 tablespoons caster sugar

Cut the jelly into pieces with scissors and put into a large measuring jug. Pour on 300 ml (¹/₂ pint) boiling water and mix with a metal spoon until the jelly has melted. Leave to cool.

Purée the strawberries in a blender or food processor or mash on a plate. Stir the strawberries into the jelly with the fromage frais and sugar and mix until smooth.

Pour the mixture into 4 jelly moulds. Chill for at least 4 hours until set.

To turn out the jellies briefly dip each mould into a bowl of hot water. Loosen the edges with your fingertips and invert the mould on to a serving plate. Holding the mould and plate together, jerk the mould to release the jelly, then remove. Top each jelly with a halved strawberry and serve.

COOK'S NOTE Try making these sundae jellies with different flavoured jelly tablets and top them with your child's favourite fruit.

163 Mini banana castles

164 Poached apricots with oatmeal cream

Preparation time:	**50 g (2 oz) soft margarine**
20 minutes	**50 g (2 oz) self-raising flour**
	25 g (1 oz) caster sugar
Cooking time:	**25 g (1 oz) ground almonds**
15 minutes	**¹/₂ teaspoon baking powder**
	1 egg
Oven temperature:	**1 ripe banana, about 125 g (4 oz)**
180°C (350°F), Gas Mark 4	**unpeeled weight**
Serves: **4**	RASPBERRY SAUCE:
	250 g (8 oz) frozen raspberries
	4 teaspoons icing sugar

Lightly grease 4 individual metal pudding moulds, each holding 150 ml (¹/₄ pint), and line the bases with rounds of greaseproof paper.

Put the margarine, flour, sugar, ground almonds and baking powder in a bowl or food processor. Add the egg and beat until smooth. Mash the banana and stir it into the mixture. Divide among the pudding moulds and level the surface.

Bake in a preheated oven, 180°C (350°F), Gas Mark 4, for 15 minutes or until well risen and golden and the tops spring back when lightly pressed with a fingertip.

Meanwhile, make the raspberry sauce. Set aside 75 g (3 oz) raspberries. Purée the rest and sieve to remove the seeds, then mix with 3 teaspoons icing sugar. Spoon on to 4 serving plates.

Loosen the puddings from their moulds, turn them out and peel off the lining paper. Stand a pudding on each plate on a pool of sauce. Arrange the reserved raspberries on the sponges and sift the remaining icing sugar over the top to decorate.

Preparation time:	**500 g (1 lb) apricots**
5 minutes	**2 tablespoons light muscovado sugar**
	¹/₂ teaspoon ground ginger
Cooking time:	**75 ml (3 fl oz) water**
10 minutes	**40 g (1¹/₂ oz) medium or coarse oatmeal**
	200 g (7 oz) Greek yogurt
Serves: **4**	**2 tablespoons double cream**
	2 tablespoons clear honey

Halve and quarter the apricots, discarding the stones. Heat the sugar, ginger and water in a saucepan until the sugar has dissolved. Add the apricots and cover the pan. Simmer gently, stirring once, for about 10 minutes or until just tender. Cool slightly, then spoon into 4 serving glasses or bowls.

Lightly toast the oatmeal in a dry frying pan over a medium heat for about 30 seconds, shaking the pan frequently. Allow to cool slightly, then stir the toasted oatmeal into the yogurt, with the cream and honey. Spoon over the fruit and serve warm. Alternatively, chill before serving if preferred.

COOK'S NOTE **Ready-to-eat dried apricots can be used instead of fresh ones. Cut 250 g (8 oz) apricots in half, then poach as above, using 200 ml (7 fl oz) water and only 1 tablespoon sugar.**

165 Plum strudel

166 Pan-fried oranges and bananas

Preparation time:
15 minutes

Cooking time:
30 minutes

Oven temperature:
200°C (400°F), Gas Mark 6

Serves: 4–6

25 g (1 oz) unsalted butter
50 g (2 oz) wholemeal breadcrumbs
½ teaspoon ground cinnamon
50 g (2 oz) ground almonds
75 g (3 oz) sultanas
50 g (2 oz) caster sugar (preferably unrefined)
3 sheets filo pastry, about 150 g (5 oz) in total
2 tablespoons sunflower oil
1 kg (2 lb) ripe plums (preferably Victoria), halved, stoned and sliced
15 g (½ oz) flaked almonds
2 teaspoons icing sugar, for dusting

Melt the butter in a frying pan, add the breadcrumbs and cinnamon and fry gently until crisp. Take off the heat and stir in the ground almonds, sultanas and sugar.

Lay a filo sheet on a clean surface and brush with a little oil. Cover with a second sheet and brush with oil. Cover with the final sheet and sprinkle with the crumb mixture to 2.5 cm (1 inch) from the edges.

Scatter the plums over the crumb mixture. Fold the 2 short ends inwards slightly over the filling then, starting from a long side, loosely roll up the strudel like a Swiss roll.

Place the roll, join side down, on a rimmed baking sheet. Brush with a little more oil and scatter with the flaked almonds. Bake in a preheated oven, 200°C (400°F), Gas Mark 6, for about 30 minutes or until golden. Leave to cool slightly, dust with icing sugar and serve cut into slices.

Preparation time:
5 minutes

Cooking time:
5 minutes

Serves: 4

2 oranges
25 g (1 oz) unsalted butter
1 cinnamon stick, halved
25 g (1 oz) light muscovado sugar
4 bananas, each cut diagonally into 4 pieces
5 tablespoons orange juice
25 g (1 oz) broken walnuts, toasted
yogurt or vanilla ice cream, to serve

Cut the peel from the oranges and remove the white pith. Thinly slice the flesh into rounds, discarding any pips but reserving the juice.

Melt the butter in a nonstick frying pan. Add the cinnamon stick and sugar and heat gently, stirring until the sugar has dissolved.

Add the bananas to the syrup and cook gently for 2 minutes, stirring frequently. Add the orange slices and juice and cook until the syrup is bubbling.

Serve warm, scattered with toasted walnuts and topped with spoonfuls of thick yogurt or scoops of good-quality vanilla ice cream.

COOK'S NOTE This recipe lends itself to flavour variations. Try adding a handful of dried fruit, such as raisins or sliced prunes, apricots, pears or mango. If you like, use different spices, such as like crushed cardamom pods, freshly grated nutmeg or allspice, or stir in some thinly sliced pieces of preserved stem ginger in syrup.

167 Easy orange cheesecake

Preparation time:
20 minutes, plus chilling

Cooking time:
5 minutes

Serves: **6–8**

50 g (2 oz) unsalted butter
2 tablespoons golden syrup
150 g (5 oz) digestive biscuit crumbs
315 g (10¹/₂ oz) can mandarin oranges in natural juice, drained
250 g (8 oz) mascarpone cheese
150 g (5 oz) fromage frais
50 g (2 oz) caster sugar
rind and juice of 1 small orange
rind and juice of 1 lime
150 ml (¹/₄ pint) double cream

Heat the butter and syrup in a nonstick saucepan until melted, stir in the biscuit crumbs and mix well. Tip the crumb mixture into the base of a springform tin and press it flat.

Arrange about three-quarters of the mandarin oranges over the crumb base. Reserve the rest for decorating.

Put the mascarpone cheese in a mixing bowl and beat to soften it. Stir in the fromage frais and sugar. Stir the orange and lime rind and juice into the cheese mixture.

In a separate bowl whip the cream until it thickens and becomes soft swirls. Gently fold into the cheese mixture, then pour the mixture into the tin and make soft wave-like shapes over the top with the back of the metal spoon.

Decorate with the remaining mandarin oranges and chill for at least 4 hours. Before serving unclip the tin and transfer the cheesecake to a serving plate.

168 Pear and hazelnut pudding

Preparation time:
10 minutes

Cooking time:
35 minutes

Oven temperature:
180°C (350°F), Gas Mark 4

Serves: **4–6**

4 ripe pears
75 g (3 oz) unsalted butter, softened
75 g (3 oz) caster sugar
25 g (1 oz) wholemeal plain flour
100 g (3¹/₂ oz) ground hazelnuts
¹/₂ teaspoon baking powder
2 eggs
1 teaspoon almond extract
1 tablespoon semi-skimmed milk
2 tablespoons roughly chopped hazelnuts
icing sugar, for dusting
Greek yogurt or single cream, to serve

Peel, halve and core the pears. Place the pear halves, cut sides up, in a shallow, ovenproof dish so they fit in a single layer with a little space around them.

Put the butter, sugar, flour, ground hazelnuts, baking powder, eggs and almond extract in a bowl and beat together for 1–2 minutes or until light and creamy. Stir in the milk. Pour the mixture over and around the pears and scatter the chopped hazelnuts over the surface.

Bake in a preheated oven, 180°C (350°F), Gas Mark 4, for about 35 minutes or until golden and just firm to the touch. Serve dusted with icing sugar and with dollops of yogurt or cream.

COOK'S NOTES Canned pears can be used instead of fresh ones, but they need to be drained thoroughly. If you can't get ground hazelnuts, grind chopped hazelnuts in a food processor or blender or use ground almonds instead.

169 Chocolate puddle pudding

Preparation time:
15 minutes

Cooking time:
15 minutes

Oven temperature:
180°C (350°F), Gas Mark 4

Serves: **4–6**

SAUCE:
2 tablespoons cocoa powder
50 g (2 oz) soft light brown sugar
250 ml (8 fl oz) boiling water

PUDDING:
75 g (3 oz) unsalted butter, softened
75 g (3 oz) soft light brown sugar
65 g (2¹/₂ oz) self-raising flour
3 tablespoons cocoa powder
3 eggs
¹/₂ teaspoon baking powder
little icing sugar, to decorate
ice cream or cream, to serve

Make the sauce. Put the cocoa and sugar into a small bowl and mix in a little of the measured boiling water to make a smooth paste. Gradually mix in the rest of the water.

Make the pudding. Rub a little of the butter all over the base and sides of a cooking dish and stand the dish on a baking sheet. In a large bowl mix together all the ingredients, except the icing sugar, until smooth.

Spoon the pudding mixture into the dish, spread the top level, then pour the cocoa sauce over the top. Bake in a preheated oven, 180°C (350°F), Gas Mark 4, for 15 minutes or until the sauce has sunk to the bottom of the dish and the pudding is well risen. Sift a little icing sugar over the pudding and serve with scoops of vanilla ice cream or a little pouring cream.

170 Raspberry and peach mallow

Preparation time:
10 minutes

Cooking time:
8 minutes

Oven temperature:
220°C (425°F), Gas Mark 7

Serves: **4**

2 ripe peaches, stoned and roughly chopped
1 tablespoon water
40 g (1¹/₂ oz) caster sugar, plus 1 tablespoon
250 g (8 oz) raspberries
2 egg whites
¹/₂ teaspoon vanilla extract
Greek yogurt, to serve (optional)

Put the peaches in a small saucepan with the water and 1 tablespoon sugar. Heat gently until the peaches are slightly softened and juicy. Stir in the raspberries and then divide the fruits among 4 large ramekins or small heatproof bowls.

Whisk the egg whites in a perfectly clean bowl until stiffly peaking. Gradually whisk in the sugar, a little at a time, until the mixture is glossy. Whisk in the vanilla extract.

Spoon the meringue over the fruits, spreading it to the edges of the dishes and piling it up in the centre. Lightly peak the meringue with the back of a spoon. Bake in a preheated oven, 220°C (425°F), Gas Mark 7, for about 5 minutes or until the meringue is golden. Keep a close eye on the meringue because it will colour quickly. Serve warm with Greek yogurt, if liked.

COOK'S TIP If you like use ripe plums, gooseberries or greengages or a combination of redcurrants and nectarines. You will probably need to add a little extra sugar for sharper fruits.

171 Nectarine and coconut crumble

172 Warm summer trifle

Preparation time:
15 minutes

Cooking time:
25 minutes

Oven temperature:
180°C (350°F), Gas Mark 4

Serves: **4–6**

750 g (1¹/₂ lb) ripe nectarines, pitted and thickly sliced
75 g (3 oz) caster sugar
100 g (3¹/₂ oz) plain flour
50 g (2 oz) unsalted butter, diced
50 g (2 oz) desiccated coconut
ice cream or pouring cream, to serve

Preparation time:
15 minutes

Cooking time:
20 minutes

Oven temperature:
160°C (325°F), Gas Mark 3

Serves: **4–6**

100 g (3¹/₂ oz) trifle sponges, plain sponge, Madeira cake or jam Swiss roll
3 tablespoons orange juice
375 g (12 oz) frozen mixed summer fruits (just thawed)
425 g (14 oz) can custard
3 egg whites
75 g (3 oz) caster sugar

Arrange the nectarines in the bottom of an ovenproof pie dish and sprinkle with 2 tablespoons sugar.

Put the rest of the sugar in a mixing bowl. Add the flour and butter and rub in with your fingertips until the mixture resembles fine breadcrumbs. Stir in the coconut.

Spoon the coconut crumble over the nectarines. Cook in a preheated oven, 180°C (350°F), Gas Mark 4, for 25 minutes or until the crumble is golden-brown. Serve warm with scoops of vanilla ice cream or cream.

Crumble the sponge into the base of an ovenproof serving dish. Drizzle the orange juice over the sponge. Add the mixed fruits and spoon the custard over the top.

Put the egg whites in a large, perfectly clean bowl. Whisk until the bowl can be turned upside down without the eggs falling out. Gradually whisk in the sugar, a spoonful at a time. Whisk for a further 1–2 minutes once all the sugar has been added until the meringue is smooth and glossy.

Spoon the meringue over the top of the custard and leave the top in large swirls. Cook in a preheated oven, 160°C (325°F), Gas Mark 3, for 20 minutes or until the meringue is golden-brown on top and all the trifle layers are heated through.

COOK'S NOTE Check the crumble after 10 minutes. Some ovens are hotter than others, and because coconut makes the crumble brown quickly you may need to cover the top with foil so that it doesn't become too dark before it is cooked.

173 Peach puff pies

174 Strawberry sorbet

Preparation time: **15 minutes**	**200 g (7 oz) ready-rolled puff pastry** **1 egg, beaten** **2 ripe peaches, pitted and chopped**
Cooking time: **10 minutes**	**2 tablespoons strawberry or apricot jam** **200 g (7 oz) crème fraîche** **125 g (4 oz) raspberries (thawed if frozen)**
Oven temperature: **200°C (400°F), Gas Mark 6**	**icing sugar, for dusting**

Makes:
12 pies

Unroll the puff pastry sheet and cut it into 12 pieces. Peel off the paper and place the pastry squares, spacing them slightly apart, on a lightly oiled baking sheet. Brush the surfaces with egg.

Mix the peaches with the jam and divide the peach and jam mixture among the pastry squares.

Bake the peach pies in a preheated oven, 200°C (400°F), Gas Mark 6, for 10 minutes or until well risen and golden. Leave to cool, then top the pies with spoonfuls of crème fraîche and the raspberries. Dust with icing sugar and serve.

Preparation time: **15 minutes, plus freezing**	**175 g (6 oz) caster sugar** **150 ml (¼ pint) water** **500 g (1 lb) strawberries, hulled**
Cooking time: **3 minutes**	**500 g (1 lb) fat-free fromage frais** **ice cream cones, to serve**

Serves: **4–6**

Put the sugar and water in a saucepan and cook gently until the sugar has dissolved. Boil for 1 minute and remove from the heat.

Purée the strawberries in a blender or food processor until smooth (there is no need to sieve) and transfer to a bowl. Whisk the fromage frais into the puréed fruit, then gradually mix in the cooled sugar syrup.

Pour the mixture into a pre-cooled ice cream machine and churn for about 45 minutes or until it is thick. Alternatively, pour the strawberry mixture into a plastic container and freeze for 3 hours.

Scoop the semi-frozen sherbet into a food processor or blender and blend until smooth. Alternatively, beat the sherbet with a fork while it is still in the plastic container.

Return to the freezer for 3 more hours or until firm enough to scoop. Serve in ice cream cones.

COOK'S NOTE Decorate some plain ice cream cones by dipping the tops into 100 g (3½ oz) melted white or plain dark chocolate. Before the chocolate sets, sprinkle it with pastel-coloured sugar strands or grated chocolate. Leave to harden, then add the sorbet or ice cream.

175 Apple snow

Preparation time:
10 minutes, plus freezing

Cooking time:
5 minutes

Serves: **4–6**

**5 large dessert apples, peeled, cored and
  thickly sliced**
4 tablespoons lemon juice
125 g (4 oz) caster sugar
300 ml (1/2 pint) water
**few drops green food colouring
  (optional)**
jelly beans, to decorate

Put the apple slices in a saucepan and add the lemon juice, sugar and water. Cover and cook gently for 5 minutes or until the apples are soft.

Leave the mixture to cool, then purée in a blender or food processor with a few drops of green food colouring (if used). Alternatively, press the mixture through a sieve into a bowl and mix in the colouring.

Pour the mixture into a shallow, stainless steel or plastic container so that the apple mixture is only about 2.5 cm (1 inch) deep. Freeze for 2 hours until the edges of the mixture are icy.

Beat the mixture with a fork until the icy edges become smooth. Freeze again for 30 minutes, then beat with the fork again. Continue beating and freezing 4 more times until the mixture looks like snow. It should take about 2 hours in all. Spoon the iced apple into bowls and decorate with jelly beans.

COOK'S NOTE A great alternative to ice cream, this 'snow' will help cool little ones on hot days.

176 Baked ice cream

Preparation time:
20 minutes

Cooking time: **2–3 minutes**

Oven temperature:
220°C (425°F), Gas Mark 7

Serves: **4**

**125 g (4 oz) sponge cake, such as
  Madeira cake**
4 teaspoons raspberry or strawberry jam
150 g (5 oz) raspberries
100 ml (3 1/2 fl oz) orange juice
2 egg whites
40 g (1 1/2 oz) caster sugar
4 large scoops vanilla ice cream

Slice the sponge cake in half and sandwich the halves together with jam. Chop the sponge into small pieces and scatter into 4 ovenproof glass ramekins, each holding about 175 ml (6 fl oz).

Add the raspberries and spoon over the orange juice. Press the mixture down gently.

Whisk the egg whites in a perfectly clean bowl until they are softly peaking when the whisk is lifted from the bowl. Gradually whisk in the sugar, a teaspoonful at a time. Whisk the mixture for about 15 seconds before adding more sugar.

Place a scoop of ice cream in each dish. Place a large spoonful of the meringue over the ice cream, spreading it so that the ice cream is completely covered. Make peaks over the meringue.

Place the dishes on a baking sheet and bake in a preheated oven, 220°C (425°F), Gas Mark 7, for 2–3 minutes or until the meringue is pale golden. Transfer the ramekins to plates and serve immediately.

177 Strawberry ice cream

178 Raspberry ripple

Preparation time:
15 minutes, plus freezing

Serves: **6**

500 g (1 lb) strawberries, hulled
4 tablespoons orange juice
175 g (6 oz) caster sugar
450 ml (³/₄ pint) whipping cream

TO DECORATE:
wild strawberries
strawberry syrup

Finely mash the strawberries and mix with the orange juice to form a smooth purée. Stir in the sugar. (If you are using an ice cream machine transfer the mixture to the machine at this point, add the cream and churn and freeze according to the manufacturer's instructions.)

Whip the cream until it forms soft peaks and fold it into the purée. Pour the mixture into a 1 kg (2 lb) loaf tin. Freeze for 1¹/₂ hours or until it is partly frozen.

Turn the mixture into a bowl, break it up with a fork and then whisk until smooth. Return the mixture to the tin and freeze for at least 5 hours until completely frozen.

Transfer to the refrigerator 30 minutes before serving and serve decorated with wild strawberries and strawberry syrup.

Preparation time:
15 minutes, plus freezing

Serves: **6**

450 ml (³/₄ pint) double cream
400 g (13 oz) can sweetened condensed milk
1 teaspoon vanilla extract
4 tablespoons raspberry jam
ice cream cones, to serve

Put the cream in a mixing bowl and whisk until it is beginning to thicken and making soft, wave-like swirls.

Stir the condensed milk and vanilla extract into the cream and transfer the mixture to a large plastic container. Freeze the mixture for 3 hours until semi-frozen.

Beat the ice cream to break up ice crystals. Scoop one-third into a second plastic container and dot with half the jam. Cover with a second layer of ice cream, the rest of the jam, then the last of the ice cream. Run a knife through the layers to create a marbled effect.

Return the ice cream to the freezer and chill for at least 3 hours or until hard enough to scoop. Serve scooped into cones.

COOK'S NOTES Homemade ice cream is more difficult to scoop than bought ice cream, especially if it has been in the freezer for a couple of days. Take it out of the freezer about 15 minutes before you need it so it can soften before scooping.

179 Peach ice cream

180 Lemon yogurt ice

Preparation time:
20 minutes, plus freezing

Cooking time:
15 minutes

Serves: **6–8**

**4 large, ripe peaches, about 750 g (1½ lb)
  in total, skinned
50 g (2 oz) icing sugar
1 tablespoon lemon juice
2 tablespoons white wine
2 teaspoons gelatine
4 egg yolks
300 ml (½ pint) double cream**

TO SERVE:
**ice cream cones dipped in melted
  chocolate
crushed pistachio nuts**

Purée the peach flesh with the sugar in a blender or food processor. Mix together the lemon juice and wine in a small bowl and sprinkle on the gelatine.

Transfer the peach purée to a large, heatproof bowl. Beat in the egg yolks and place the bowl over a pan of gently simmering water and stir until it thickens.

Stand the bowl with the gelatine in a shallow pan of hot water and leave until it dissolves. Stir the gelatine into the peach mixture and leave to cool. (If you are using an ice cream machine transfer the mixture to the machine at this point, add the cream and churn and freeze according to the manufacturer's instructions.)

Whip the cream until it forms soft peaks, then fold it into the peach mixture. Transfer it to a freezer container, cover and freeze until firm, beating twice at hourly intervals.

Serve with ice cream cones dipped in melted plain dark chocolate and crushed pistachio nuts.

Preparation time:
10 minutes, plus freezing

Cooking time:
2 minutes

Serves: **4**

**175 g (6 oz) caster sugar
150 ml (¼ pint) water
finely grated rind and juice of 2 large
  lemons
500 ml (17 fl oz) natural yogurt**

Put the sugar and water in a large pan and heat gently, stirring, until the sugar has dissolved. Leave to cool. Whisk in the lemon rind, juice and yogurt until the mixture is smooth.

To freeze by hand pour the mixture into a shallow freezer container and freeze for 3–4 hours, until it is frozen around the edges and slushy in the centre. Turn into a bowl and whisk until it is smooth. Return to the container and re-freeze until softly frozen. Repeat the freezing and whisking process until the yogurt ice has a creamy consistency.

To freeze in an ice cream machine, churn until the mixture is thick and creamy then transfer to a freezer container and freeze.

About 30 minutes before serving transfer the yogurt ice to the refrigerator to soften slightly.

COOK'S NOTES Serve this as a lighter, more refreshing alternative to ice cream or as a long, cooling summer drink, scooped into glasses and topped up with lemonade.

181 Old-fashioned vanilla ice cream

182 Chocolate ice cream

Preparation time:
20 minutes, plus freezing

Cooking time:
30 minutes

Serves: **6**

300 ml (½ pint) single cream
1 vanilla pod
4 egg yolks
50 g (2 oz) caster sugar
300 ml (½ pint) double or whipping cream

CARAMEL SAUCE:
75 g (3 oz) granulated sugar
4 tablespoons water
150 ml (¼ pint) double cream

Preparation time:
20 minutes, plus freezing

Cooking time:
10 minutes

Serves: **4**

300 ml (½ pint) double cream
2 tablespoons milk
50 g (2 oz) icing sugar, sifted
½ teaspoon vanilla extract
125 g (4 oz) plain dark chocolate, chopped
2 tablespoons single cream
chocolate sauce, to serve (optional)

Make the sauce. Put the sugar in a small, heavy-based saucepan and heat, stirring until golden-brown. Remove from the heat and add the water. Return to the heat and stir until smooth. Leave to cool. Lightly whip the cream and beat in the caramel until smooth.

Put the single cream and vanilla pod in a heavy-based saucepan over a low heat and bring to just below boiling point. Remove from the heat and leave to infuse.

Meanwhile, put the egg yolks and sugar in a heatproof bowl and set over a pan of simmering water. Stir until thick and creamy. Gradually stir in the single cream, discarding the vanilla pod. Continue stirring for 15 minutes or until the custard coats the back of the spoon. Remove from the heat and leave to cool.

Pour the vanilla mixture into a freezer container, cover and freeze for about 45 minutes or until slushy. Whip the cream until it just holds its shape. Remove the vanilla mixture from the freezer, beat thoroughly and fold in the cream. Return the mixture to the container, cover and freeze for a further 45 minutes. Beat again until smooth.

Freeze the ice cream for at least 1–2 hours. Transfer to the refrigerator for about 30 minutes to soften slightly before serving. Decorate with the caramel sauce.

Put the double cream and milk in a bowl and whisk until just stiff. Stir in the icing sugar and vanilla extract and pour the mixture into a shallow freezer container. Freeze for 30 minutes or until the ice cream begins to set around the edges.

Put the chocolate and single cream in a heatproof bowl set over a pan of gently simmering water. Stir gently until melted and smooth. Set aside to cool.

Remove the ice cream from the freezer and spoon into a bowl. Add the melted chocolate and quickly stir it through the ice cream with a fork. Return the ice cream to the freezer container, cover and freeze until set.

Transfer the ice cream to the refrigerator 30 minutes before serving so that it softens slightly. Serve with chocolate sauce, if liked.

COOK'S NOTES Don't be tempted to make this ice cream in an ice cream machine – it needs to be made by hand for a lovely smooth texture and rich chocolate flavour.

183 Peppermint candy ice cream

184 Dark chocolate fondue

Preparation time:
20 minutes, plus freezing

Cooking time:
5 minutes

Serves: 4

4 egg yolks
50 g (2 oz) caster sugar
1 teaspoon cornflour
300 ml (1/2 pint) milk
50 g (2 oz) peppermint candy canes or peppermint rock, crushed, plus extra to decorate (optional)
300 ml (1/2 pint) whipping cream

Beat the egg yolks in a bowl with the sugar, cornflour and a little of the milk until smooth. Bring the remaining milk to the boil in a heavy-based saucepan. Pour the milk over the egg yolk mixture, whisking well until combined. Return the mixture to the saucepan and cook gently, stirring, until it is thick enough to coat the back of the spoon.

Transfer the custard to a bowl, cover with a circle of greaseproof paper to prevent a skin from forming and leave to cool. Chill until cold. (If you are using an ice cream machine transfer the mixture to the machine at this point, add the crushed peppermint and cream and churn and freeze according to the manufacturer's instructions.)

Lightly whip the cream and fold it into the custard with the crushed peppermint. Turn into a freezer container, cover and freeze until the mixture has frozen around the edges. Remove from the freezer. Transfer to a bowl and whisk lightly.

Return to the freezer until the mixture has frozen around the edges. Repeat the whisking and freezing once or twice more, then freeze the ice cream until ready to serve.

Transfer the ice cream to the refrigerator about 30 minutes before serving to soften slightly. Scoop into glasses and sprinkle with extra crushed peppermint candy, if liked.

Preparation time:
5 minutes

Cooking time:
10 minutes

Serves: 4

250 g (8 oz) plain dark chocolate, finely chopped
15 g (1/2 oz) unsalted butter
2 tablespoons double cream
40 g (11/2 oz) stem ginger, chopped

TO SERVE:
fresh strawberries
brandy snaps or marshmallows

Fill a fondue pot one-third full of boiling water. Place the porcelain liner in the pot and heat gently on the hob. Put the chocolate in the pot with the butter, cream and stem ginger. Place over a low heat and stir occasionally until the chocolate has melted.

Transfer the fondue pot to its tabletop burner and keep warm over a low heat. Serve immediately with fresh strawberries and brandy snaps or marshmallows.

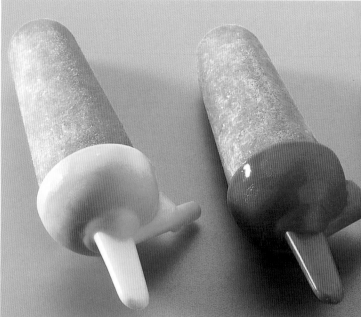

Preparation time:
5–15 minutes, plus freezing

Cooking time:
0–5 minutes

Makes:
4 lollies

SPOTTY ORANGE LOLLIES:
**200ml (7 fl oz) orange juice
small pack jelly tots**

BUSY BEES:
**125 g (4 oz) blackberries or blackcurrants
1 tablespoon caster sugar
1 tablespoon water
2 peaches or nectarines, stone removed**

SPOTTY ORANGE LOLLIES:
Pour the orange juice into a 4-section lolly mould and freeze until mushy. Drop the Jelly Tots into the semi-frozen mixture. Freeze and unmould.

BUSY BEES:
Put the blackberries or blackcurrants into a small pan with the caster sugar and water. Cover and cook for 5 minutes until just soft. Purée until smooth, then sieve and leave to cool. Purée the peaches or nectarines until smooth, then sieve.

Spoon 1 teaspoon peach or nectarine purée into the base of 4 lolly moulds. Freeze until solid, then spoon 1 teaspoon of blackberry or blackcurrant purée on top. Freeze again until solid. Repeat until the moulds are full. Freeze and unmould.

Preparation time:
10 minutes, plus freezing

Makes:
8 lollies

**625 g (1¼ lb) wedge of watermelon
finely grated rind and juice of 2 limes
150 ml (¼ pint) apple juice
2 tablespoons caster sugar**

Scoop the red melon flesh and black seeds away from the green skin and into a food processor or blender. Blend briefly so that the fruit is puréed but the seeds are still whole. Sieve the melon flesh to remove the seeds.

Stir the lime rind and juice into the melon purée together with the apple juice and sugar.

Pour the melon mixture into the sections of the ice lolly mould. Add the tops and freeze for at least 4 hours.

To serve, dip the lolly moulds into hot water for a count of 10, then flex the handles and remove the lollies from their moulds.

COOK'S NOTES Make strawberry-flavoured lollies by puréeing 150 g (5 oz) strawberries in a blender or food processor. Press through a sieve to remove the seeds. Mix with 2 x 40 g (1½ oz) pots of strawberry fromage frais. Pour into a 4-section mould. Freeze and unmould as above.

187 Fresh apple lollies

188 Fresh fruit lollies

Preparation time:
**10–15 minutes, plus
freezing**

**500 g (1 lb) cooking apples, peeled, cored
and chopped
clear honey**

Cooking time:
10–20 minutes

Makes:
4 lollies

Put the apples in a saucepan and add just enough water to cover the bottom of the pan. Simmer gently for 10–20 minutes until tender.

Purée the apples in a food processor or blender or press them through a sieve to make a smooth purée. Sweeten to taste with honey.

Leave the purée to cool, then pour it into lolly moulds or ice cube trays and freeze until mushy. Add sticks and return to the freezer until completely set.

To serve, dip the lolly moulds into hot water for a count of 10, then flex the handles and remove the lollies from their moulds.

Preparation time:
5 minutes, plus freezing

**375 g (12 oz) pineapple, chopped
375 g (12 oz) blackcurrants, fresh or
frozen**

Makes:
4 lollies

Purée or juice the fruit, alternating the pineapple with the blackcurrants to ensure that the juice flows freely.

Pour the juice into 4 small lolly moulds and freeze immediately, before all the goodness has had a chance to slip away. Add the plastic handle tops and freeze until solid.

To serve, dip the lolly moulds into hot water for a count of 10, then flex the handles and remove the lollies from the moulds.

COOK'S NOTES Instead of apples you could try simmering other
fruit to make purées, such as apricots, plums, peaches or blackcurrants.
Raspberries, strawberries, blueberries, kiwifruit and melon, can be
blended uncooked with unsweetened apple juice and then frozen.

7 Bakes

189 Cranberry muffins   190 Muffin mania

Preparation time: **10 minutes**	**100 g (3¹/₂ oz) white self-raising flour** **100 g (3¹/₂ oz) wholemeal self-raising flour**
Cooking time: **15 minutes**	**1 teaspoon baking powder** **1 teaspoon ground ginger** **75 g (3 oz) medium oatmeal**
Oven temperature: **200°C (400°F), Gas Mark 6**	**125 g (4 oz) caster sugar** **75 g (3 oz) dried cranberries** **4 tablespoons light olive oil**
Makes: **12 muffins**	**300 ml (¹/₂ pint) natural yogurt** **2 eggs** **extra oatmeal, for sprinkling**

Sift the flours, baking powder and ginger into a bowl, tipping in the grains left in the sieve. Stir in the oatmeal, sugar and dried cranberries.

In another bowl beat together the oil, yogurt and eggs until blended. Add to the dry ingredients and fold in until just incorporated, but with some dry grains still visible.

Line a 12-section muffin tin with paper muffin cases. Spoon the mixture into the paper cases and sprinkle with a little extra oatmeal. Bake in a preheated oven, 200°C (400°F), Gas Mark 6, for about 15 minutes or until just firm to the touch. Transfer to a wire rack to cool.

Preparation time: **10 minutes**	**200 g (7 oz) self-raising flour** **¹/₂ teaspoon baking powder** **2 eggs, beaten**
Cooking time: **15 minutes**	**5 tablespoons sunflower oil** **5 tablespoons full-fat milk** **1 teaspoon vanilla extract**
Oven temperature: **200°C (400°F), Gas Mark 6**	**2 ripe bananas, about 325 g (11 oz) unpeeled weight** **100 g (3¹/₂ oz) milk chocolate dots**
Makes: **12 muffins**	

Sift the flour and baking powder together into a mixing bowl. Beat the eggs, oil, milk and vanilla extract together in a separate bowl.

Mash the bananas on a plate, using a fork, then add to the flour with the egg mixture. Mix the ingredients together briefly until only just mixed. Stir in the chocolate dots.

Line a 12-section muffin tray with paper muffin cases. Spoon the mixture into the paper cases and bake in a preheated oven, 200°C (400°F), Gas Mark 6, for 15 minutes or until the muffins are well risen and the tops spring back when lightly pressed with the fingertips. Transfer to a wire rack to cool.

COOK'S NOTES Because they don't keep well, it's best to freeze any muffins that won't be eaten on the day they are made. Simply remove them from the freezer as required, for snacks and lunchboxes. If you can't buy dried cranberries use dried blueberries, dried cherries, raisins or sultanas.

191 Coconut and blueberry cakes

Preparation time: **10 minutes**	**125 g (4 oz) unsalted butter, softened** **125 g (4 oz) light muscovado sugar** **2 eggs**
Cooking time: **20–25 minutes**	**50 g (2 oz) white self-raising flour** **50 g (2 oz) wholemeal self-raising flour** **½ teaspoon baking powder**
Oven temperature: **180°C (350°F), Gas Mark 4**	**1 teaspoon vanilla extract** **50 g (2 oz) desiccated coconut** **150 g (5 oz) blueberries**
Makes: **12 cakes**	

Put the butter, sugar and eggs in a mixing bowl. Sift the flours and baking powder into the bowl, tipping in the grains left in the sieve. Add the vanilla extract. Beat with a hand-held electric whisk for 2 minutes or until light and creamy. Stir in the coconut and blueberries.

Line a 12-section muffin tin with paper muffin cases and spoon the mixture into the cases. Bake in a preheated oven, 180°C (350°F), Gas Mark 4, for 20–25 minutes or until risen and just firm. Transfer to a wire rack to cool.

COOK'S NOTES The cakes can be stored in an airtight container for up to 3–4 days. They also freeze well so you can pop them in a freezer bag or container and take out individual cakes as required. Defrost at room temperature for an hour or so or briefly pop in the microwave if serving at once. As an alternative to blueberries use quartered fresh cherries or dried blueberries or cranberries.

192 Chocolate orange brownies

Preparation time: **15–20 minutes**	**150 g (5 oz) orange-flavoured dark** ** chocolate or plain dark chocolate and** ** 1 teaspoon orange essence**
Cooking time: **25–30 minutes**	**150 g (5 oz) unsalted butter** **250 g (8 oz) caster sugar** **4 eggs**
Oven temperature: **180°C (350°F), Gas Mark 4**	**finely grated rind of 1 orange** **175 g (6 oz) plain flour** **1 teaspoon baking powder**
Makes: **16 brownies**	**150 g (5 oz) milk chocolate, roughly** ** chopped** **75 g (3 oz) macadamia nuts, roughly** ** chopped** **pinch of salt**

Put the plain chocolate and butter in a heavy-based pan over a low heat until just melted. Remove from the heat, stir in the sugar and set aside to cool a little. Pour the melted chocolate into a large bowl and beat in the eggs, orange rind and orange essence (if used).

Sift the flour, salt and baking powder into the bowl and fold in to the chocolate mixture, along with the milk chocolate chunks and macadamia nuts. Pour the mixture into a greased and lined baking tin, about 20 x 30 x 5 cm (8 x 12 x 2 inches).

Cook in a preheated oven, 180°C (350°F), Gas Mark 4, for 25–30 minutes or until set but not too firm. Allow to cool in the pan, then cut into squares and serve.

193 Carob and nut brownies 　 194 Fruity crumble squares

Preparation time:
15 minutes

Cooking time:
25–30 minutes

Oven temperature:
350°F (180°C), Gas Mark 4

Makes:
12 brownies

125 g (4 oz) unsalted butter
5 tablespoons clear honey
1¹/₂ teaspoons vanilla extract
2 eggs, lightly beaten
125 g (4 oz) wholemeal self-raising flour
2 teaspoons carob powder
125 g (4 oz) carob bar, broken into small
**　pieces**
50 g (2 oz) chopped walnuts, hazelnuts or
**　pistachios**

Preparation time:
15 minutes

Cooking time:
30 minutes

Oven temperature:
180°C (350°F), Gas Mark 4

Makes:
12 squares

175 g (6 oz) unsalted butter, diced
250 g (8 oz) plain flour
2 tablespoons cornflour
75 g (3 oz) caster sugar
1 small dessert apple
100 g (3¹/₂ oz) exotic ready-to-eat dried
**　fruits or just apricots**
icing sugar, to dust

Cream the butter in a large mixing bowl. Add the honey, vanilla extract and egg and beat until creamy. Mix in all the other ingredients and combine well.

Spoon the mixture into a lightly greased, 18 cm (7 inch) nonstick baking tin and smooth the top. Bake in a preheated oven, 180°C (350°F), Gas Mark 4, for 25–30 minutes. The mixture will puff up at first then drop to form a crust. Test it with a skewer; when it is not too runny inside, it is done.

Leave the cake to cool for 5 minutes in the tin, then cut it into bars and leave to cool completely on a wire rack.

Put the butter in a large bowl with the flour, cornflour and sugar. Rub in the butter with your fingertips until the mixture resembles fine breadcrumbs. Reserve 125 g (4 oz) of the crumbs.

Squeeze the rest of the crumbs together with your hands to make a ball, then press the mixture into the base of an ungreased baking tin.

Grate the apple (still with its skin on) over the shortbread mixture in the tin, discarding the core. Cut the dried fruit into pieces and scatter them over the apple. Sprinkle with the reserved crumb mixture.

Bake in a preheated oven, 180°C (350°F), Gas Mark 4, for 30 minutes or until the top is lightly browned. Leave to cool in the tin for 15 minutes, cut into 12 pieces and leave to cool completely. Decorate with sifted icing sugar.

COOK'S NOTES To freeze the brownies place them in a container in layers separated by freezer paper or wrapped in foil. Defrost at room temperature for 1 hour, then reheat at 200°C (400°F), Gas Mark 6, for 10 minutes, if liked. They can be frozen for up to 4 months.

195 Hot cross buns

Preparation time:
1 hour, plus proving

Cooking time:
20 minutes

Oven temperature:
190°C (375°F), Gas Mark 4

Makes:
12 buns

375 g (12 oz) strong bread flour
150 ml (¹/₄ pint) milk
4 tablespoons water
25 g (1 oz) fresh yeast
1 teaspoon caster sugar
1 teaspoon salt
¹/₂ teaspoon ground cinnamon
50 g (2 oz) caster sugar
50 g (2 oz) unsalted butter, melted
1 egg, beaten
175 g (6 oz) currants
75 g (3 oz) mixed peel, chopped
50 g (2 oz) shortcrust pastry

Put 50 g (2 oz) flour in a small bowl. Warm the milk and water and blend in the yeast and 1 teaspoon sugar. Mix this into the flour and leave in a warm place to froth for 15 minutes. Sift the remaining flour, salt, cinnamon, and sugar into a large bowl.

Add the butter to the yeast mixture with the beaten egg. Stir this into the flour. Add the currants and candied peel and mix. Turn out the dough on a lightly floured surface and knead well. Put it into an oiled polythene bag and allow to rise for 1–1¹/₂ hours at room temperature until doubled in size. Turn on to a floured surface and knock back.

Divide the dough into 12 and shape into round buns. Place the buns, spaced well apart, on a floured baking sheet. Cover and put in a warm place to rise for 20–30 minutes or until doubled in size.

Roll out the pastry thinly and cut 24 thin strips about 8 cm (3 inches) long. When the buns have risen, damp the pastry strips and lay 2 across each bun to make a cross. Bake the buns in a preheated oven, 190°C (375°F), Gas Mark 4, for 20 minutes or until they are golden-brown and firm to the touch. Glaze with a little caster sugar mixed into warm milk, if liked.

196 Lemony polenta cake

Preparation time:
15 minutes

Cooking time:
35 minutes

Oven temperature:
180°C (350°F), Gas Mark 4

Makes:
12 squares

150 ml (¹/₄ pint) light olive oil
175 g (6 oz) caster sugar
125 g (4 oz) ground almonds
2 eggs
1 teaspoon vanilla extract
finely grated rind and juice of 4 lemons
175 g (6 oz) instant polenta
1 teaspoon baking powder

Grease and line an 18 cm (7 inch) square cake tin with greaseproof paper or nonstick baking paper. Put the oil, 125 g (4 oz) of the sugar, the ground almonds, eggs and vanilla extract in a mixing bowl. Add the rind and juice of 2 lemons, the polenta and baking powder and beat well with a wooden spoon until the ingredients are evenly mixed.

Pour the mixture into the prepared tin. Bake in a preheated oven at 180°C (350°F) Gas Mark 4 for about 35 minutes until just firm to the touch.

Meanwhile, mix together the remaining sugar, lemon rind and juice. Remove the cake from the oven and immediately spoon the lemon sugar mixture over the surface. Leave to cool in the tin.

Cut the cake into 12 squares. It can be stored in an airtight container for up to 4 days.

COOK'S NOTES Lemons are very high in vitamin C, which is essential for a healthy immune system. Vitamin C helps to combat colds, coughs and sore throats. Olive oil is a healthier alternative to butter and margarine in cake recipes because it is high in beneficial monounsaturated fats, but low in potentially harmful saturated fats. The essential fatty acids in olive oil help protect body cells and facilitate the absorption of some nutrients.

Preparation time:	100 g (3¹/₂ oz) unsalted butter
15 minutes	100 g (3¹/₂ oz) light muscovado sugar
	5 tablespoons clear honey
Cooking time:	375 g (12 oz) porridge oats
25 minutes	75 g (3 oz) ready-to-eat dried prunes, chopped
Oven temperature:	75 g (3 oz) ready-to-eat dried apricots, chopped
180°C (350°F), Gas Mark 4	75 g (3 oz) raisins or sultanas
Makes:	2 eggs
15–20 flapjacks	

Preparation time:	150 g (5 oz) unsalted butter
15 minutes	75 g (3 oz) raw brown cane sugar
	75 g (3 oz) blackstrap molasses
Cooking time:	250 g (8 oz) porridge oats
30–35 minutes	25 g (1 oz) dried fruit (such as apricots, prunes or sour cherries), chopped
Oven temperature:	
190°C (375°F), Gas Mark 5	
Makes:	
12 flapjacks	

Melt the butter with the sugar and honey in a small saucepan. Remove from the heat and stir in the oats, prunes, apricots and raisins or sultanas until evenly mixed. Beat in the eggs.

Turn the mixture into a shallow, lightly greased 28 x 23 cm (11 x 9 inch) baking tin and level the surface. Bake in a preheated oven, 180°C (350°F), Gas Mark 4, for 20 minutes or until turning pale golden. Leave in the tin until almost cold, then cut into fingers and leave to cool on a wire rack.

Put the butter, sugar and molasses into a saucepan and heat until the butter has melted. Mix in the oats and dried fruit and stir thoroughly.

Press the mixture into a shallow, lightly greased 20 cm (8 inch) square tin and smooth the surface. Bake in a preheated oven, 190°C (375°F), Gas Mark 5, for 25–30 minutes or until the flapjack is set and golden-brown.

Mark the flapjack into portions while still warm and leave in the tin for about 5 minutes. Remove them from the tin and leave to cool on a wire rack.

COOK'S NOTES The flapjacks can be stored in an airtight container in a cool place for up to 5 days. Other dried fruits, such as chopped figs or dates, can be used instead of those listed above. For an extra tang, add the grated rind of 1 lemon with the melted butter.

199 Chocolate crunch crisps

200 Gluten-free owl cookies

Preparation time:
10 minutes, plus chilling

Cooking time:
5 minutes

Makes:
20 crisps

125 g (4 oz) unsalted butter
2 tablespoons golden syrup
25 g (1 oz) cocoa powder
250 g (8 oz) puffed rice or millet
125 g (4 oz) dried cranberries or raisins

Put the butter and syrup in a heavy-based saucepan and heat, stirring, until the butter melts.

Add a little of the syrup mixture to the cocoa powder and mix to form a smooth paste. Return the paste to the saucepan and blend well. Add the puffed rice or millet and cranberries or raisins and stir carefully until evenly coated.

Spoon the mixture into 20 paper sweet cases. Chill until set.

COOK'S NOTES Use 50 g (2 oz) desiccated coconut instead of cocoa powder and corn or millet flakes instead of puffed rice or millet, if you prefer.

Preparation time:
15–20 minutes, plus chilling

Cooking time:
8–10 minutes

Oven temperature:
180°C (350°F), Gas Mark 4

Makes:
10 biscuits

175 g (6 oz) rice flour, plus extra for dusting
1 teaspoon baking powder
75 g (3 oz) unsalted butter, softened
50 g (2 oz) raw brown cane sugar
few drops of vanilla extract
15 g (½ oz) cocoa powder
pinch of bicarbonate of soda
20 raisins

Sift together the flour and baking powder. Cream the butter until it is light and fluffy and beat in the sugar and vanilla extract.

Mix the cocoa powder with a little water and add the bicarbonate of soda to the paste.

Add the flour and baking powder to the creamed butter and stir to blend. Put two-thirds of the mixture on a lightly floured surface. Blend the cocoa mixture into the remaining one-third. Shape both mixtures into sausages and chill for 30–60 minutes.

Divide the pale dough in half and roll out each piece to a rectangle, 10 x 12 cm (4 x 5 inches). Divide the cocoa dough in half and roll each piece into a 12 cm (5 inch) sausage. Put one piece of dark dough on a piece of pale dough and roll up. Repeat with the other pieces, then chill for a further 1–2 hours.

Cut the dough into slices 5 cm (2 inches) thick. Place 2 circles side by side and press lightly together. Pinch the top corners to form ears and add raisins for eyes. Bake in a preheated oven, 180°C (350°F), Gas Mark 4, for 8–10 minutes. Transfer to a wire rack to cool.

201 Noughts and crosses

202 Animal magic

Preparation time:
15 minutes

Cooking time:
10 minutes

Oven temperature:
190°C (375°F), Gas Mark 5

Makes:
20 biscuits

75 g (3 oz) wholemeal flour (or half wholemeal and half white flour)
75 g (3 oz) butter, diced
75 g (3 oz) medium Cheddar cheese, grated
1 egg, separated
1 tablespoon sesame seeds (optional)

Put the flour in a bowl, add the butter and rub in with your fingertips until the mixture resembles fine breadcrumbs. Stir in the cheese, then mix in the egg yolk to make a smooth dough.

Gently knead the dough and roll it out on a lightly floured surface to 5 mm (¼ inch) thick. Cut out rounds with a 6 cm (2½ inch) plain round cutter. From these, cut noughts with a 3 cm (1¼ inch) plain round cutter. Carefully lift the noughts on to a large, nonstick baking sheet.

Draw a broad cross on a piece of card, about 6 cm (2½ inches) high. Cut it out and use it as a template to cut crosses from the dough. Lift the crosses on to the baking sheet. Re-roll the trimmings to cut out more shapes.

Brush with egg white and sprinkle with sesame seeds (if used). Bake in a preheated oven, 190°C (375°F), Gas Mark 5, for 10 minutes or until golden. Leave to cool on the baking sheet. Store the biscuits in an airtight tin and eat within 2 days.

Preparation time:
20 minutes, plus chilling

Cooking time:
10 minutes

Makes:
16 biscuits

75 g (3 oz) unsalted butter
3 tablespoons golden syrup
200 g (7 oz) plain dark chocolate, chopped
100 g (3½ oz) puffed rice
50 g (2 oz) white chocolate, chopped

Brush 16 animal-shaped biscuit cutters with oil and place them on a large, lightly oiled baking sheet.

Put the butter, syrup and plain chocolate in a saucepan and heat gently, stirring occasionally, until melted. Take off the heat and add the cereal, stirring to make sure it is well coated in chocolate.

Spoon the chocolate mixture into the animal cutters and press the mixture down well. Chill until firm. Free the edges of the biscuits with a small knife or by flexing the cutters and remove.

Melt the white chocolate in a heatproof bowl over a pan of just boiled water. Spoon it into a piping bag and pipe features on the animals. Leave to harden for 30 minutes before serving.

COOK'S NOTES If you do not have enough animal cutters, spoon the remaining mixture into paper cases. Alternatively, press the chocolate mixture into an oiled 30 x 20 x 4 cm (12 x 8 x 1½ inch) loose-bottomed cake tin or foil-lined baking tin. Chill and cut into small squares, triangles or rounds. Serve in paper cake cases.

Preparation time:
20 minutes

Cooking time:
1¹/₄–1¹/₂ hours

Oven temperature:
**110°C (225°F),
Gas Mark ¹/₄**

Makes:
40 meringues

2 egg whites
100 g (3¹/₂ oz) caster sugar
few drops of food colouring (optional)

Preparation time:
10 minutes, plus cooling

Cooking time:
10–15 minutes

Oven temperature:
180°C (350°F), Gas Mark 4

Makes:
10–12 biscuits

100 g (3¹/₂ oz) unsalted butter
100 g (3¹/₂ oz) light brown sugar
100 g (3¹/₂ oz) golden syrup
225 g (7¹/₂ oz) plain flour
1 teaspoon bicarbonate of soda
1 teaspoon ground ginger

Whisk the egg whites in a large, perfectly clean bowl until stiff, but not dry. Gradually whisk in the sugar, a teaspoonful at a time, and continue whisking until smooth and glossy.

Spoon half the mixture into a piping bag fitted with a large, plain tube. Pipe numerals, about 8 cm (3 inches) high, on a lined and lightly oiled baking sheet. Colour the remaining meringue with a few drops of colouring, if liked, and pipe numbers on a second baking sheet.

Bake in a preheated oven, 110°C (225°F), Gas Mark ¹/₄, for 1¹/₄–1¹/₂ hours or until the meringue numerals may be lifted off the paper easily. Leave to cool on the baking sheets. Store the meringues in an airtight tin lined with greaseproof or nonstick baking paper for up to 4 days.

Put the butter, sugar and syrup in a saucepan and heat gently, stirring, until the butter has melted. Leave to cool for 5 minutes.

Sift the flour, bicarbonate of soda and ginger into the saucepan. Mix together to form a smooth, soft dough.

Dot teaspoonfuls of the mixture over a lightly floured surface. Allow to cool slightly, then roll each spoonful in your hand to make a smooth, round ball. Arrange the balls, spaced slightly apart, on lightly oiled baking sheets.

Bake the biscuits in a preheated oven, 180°C (350°F), Gas Mark 4, for 8–10 minutes or until the tops have cracked and are just beginning to brown. Leave to cool on the baking sheets for 2 minutes. Loosen with the palette knife and transfer to a wire rack.

COOK'S NOTES If you do not have a nylon piping bag and tube, make a large greaseproof paper piping bag and snip off the tip. Alternatively, use a strong polythene freezer bag with one of the corners snipped off.

205 Healthy sweet bread

206 Focaccia

Preparation time:
15 minutes, plus standing

Cooking time:
40–50 minutes

Oven temperature:
160°C (325°F), Gas Mark 3

Makes:
1 loaf

125 g (4 oz) fine bulgar wheat
2 eggs
150 ml (5 fl oz) vegetable oil
125 g (4 oz) honey
1 teaspoon vanilla extract
375 g (12 oz) coarsely grated courgette,
   carrot, apple or squash (or any
   combination of the 4)
250 g (8 oz) wholemeal flour
1½ teaspoons ground cinnamon
2 teaspoons baking soda
125 g (4 oz) sultanas, dried apricots, sour
   cherries or raisins

Put the bulgar wheat in a large bowl and cover with boiling water. Leave to stand for 30 minutes, then drain.

Beat the eggs until they are light and foamy, then add the oil, honey, vanilla, grated fruit and/or vegetables and the bulgar wheat.

Sift the flour into a bowl and add the cinnamon, baking soda and dried fruit. Add the dry ingredients to the egg mixture and combine well.

Spoon the mixture a lightly oiled 1 kg (2 lb) loaf tin or a rectangular baking tin. Bake in a preheated oven, 160°C (325°F), Gas Mark 3, for 40–50 minutes or until a skewer comes out clean when inserted into the centre of the loaf.

COOK'S NOTES To freeze allow the loaf to cool, then wrap it in foil or freezer paper. Defrost in its wrapping at room temperature for 2–3 hours and slice while partially frozen to prevent crumbling. It will freeze for up to 4 months.

Preparation time:
15 minutes, plus proving

Cooking time:
15 minutes

Oven temperature:
200°C (400°F), Gas Mark 6

Makes:
3 loaves

750 g (1½ lb) strong plain bread flour,
   plus extra for kneading
7 g (¼ oz) sachet fast-action dried yeast
3 teaspoons caster sugar
2 teaspoons salt
9 tablespoons olive oil
450 ml (¾ pint) lukewarm water
6 pieces sun-dried tomatoes, chopped
few stems rosemary, chopped
few black olives, pitted
coarse sea salt (optional)

Put the flour, yeast, sugar and salt in a large bowl. Add 3 tablespoons oil and gradually mix in the water. Use your hands to make a soft but not sticky dough.

Turn out the dough on to a lightly floured surface and knead it for 5 minutes or until it is smooth and elastic. Return the dough to the bowl, cover with clingfilm and put in a warm place for 45–60 minutes or until the dough has doubled in size.

Transfer the dough to a lightly floured surface and knead again until smooth. Cut the dough into 3 and pat each piece into a rough oval, about 23 cm (9 inches) across. Place on large, lightly oiled baking sheets. Make dents over each loaf by pressing the end of a wooden spoon into the dough.

Press the pieces of sun-dried tomatoes and rosemary into the holes in the bread along with the olives. Leave to rise in a warm place for about 20–30 minutes or until about half as big again.

Spoon 1 tablespoon of olive oil over each piece of bread and sprinkle with salt (if used). Bake in a preheated oven, 200°C (400°F), Gas Mark 6, for 15 minutes or until the loaves are golden-brown and sound hollow when tapped with your fingers. Spoon the rest of the oil over the bread. Serve warm or cold, torn into strips, with soup or salad.

207 Cheese and chive bread

Preparation time:	**250 g (8 oz) self-raising flour, plus extra**
20 minutes	**for kneading**
	40 g (1½ oz) butter, diced
Cooking time:	**125 g (4 oz) Cheddar cheese, grated**
15 minutes	**4 tablespoons chopped chives**
	1 egg, beaten
Oven temperature:	**1 teaspoon Dijon mustard**
200°C (400°F), Gas Mark 6	**150 ml (¼ pint) milk**
	oil, for greasing
Makes:	**salt and pepper**
6 rolls	

Put the flour, salt and pepper in a large mixing bowl. Add the butter to the bowl and rub in with your fingertips until the mixture resembles fine breadcrumbs.

Add the cheese and chives to the bowl and mix together. Add all but about 2 teaspoons of the egg to the flour mixture. Add the mustard, then gradually mix in the milk to make a soft but not sticky dough.

Turn out the dough on a lightly floured surface and knead until smooth. Pat it into a circle about 18 cm (7 inches) across, cut it into 6 segments and place them, spaced slightly apart, on a lightly oiled baking sheet.

Brush the tops of the rolls with the remaining egg and bake in a preheated oven, 200°C (400°F), Gas Mark 6, for 15 minutes or until well risen and golden. Serve warm or cold.

COOK'S NOTES This bread is delicious served warm or cold with butter, and also makes a great accompaniment to hot soup on a cold day.

208 Cheesy spirals

Preparation time:	**500 g (1 lb) strong plain bread flour, plus**
20 minutes, plus proving	**extra for kneading**
	1 teaspoon salt
Cooking time:	**2 teaspoons fast-action dried yeast**
20–25 minutes	**2 teaspoons caster sugar**
	300 ml (½ pint) lukewarm water
Oven temperature:	
200°C (400°F), Gas Mark 6	FILLING:
	3 teaspoons pesto
Makes:	**3 tablespoons tomato ketchup**
12 rolls	**2 tablespoons olive oil**
	2 tomatoes, finely chopped
	150 g (5 oz) Cheddar, mozzarella or
	Gruyère cheese, grated

Put the flour, salt, yeast and sugar in a large mixing bowl. Gradually mix the water into the flour, then shape it with your hands into a soft but not sticky dough.

Turn out the dough on to a lightly floured surface and knead for 10 minutes or until it is smooth and elastic. Roll it out to a rectangle about 40 x 25 cm (16 x 10 inches).

Make the filling. Mix together the pesto, ketchup and oil in a small bowl and spread it over the dough. Sprinkle the tomatoes over the pesto and top with the cheese.

Roll up the dough, starting with one of the long edges, and cut it into 12 thick slices. Arrange the spirals, side by side and cut side uppermost, in a lightly oiled roasting tin. If they look squashed, open out the spirals with the tip of a knife. Cover with lightly oiled clingfilm and leave in a warm place for 45–60 minutes or until well risen.

Bake in a preheated oven, 200°C (400°F), Gas Mark 6, for 20–25 minutes or until well risen and golden and the bread sounds hollow when tapped with your fingertips. Leave to cool in the tin and serve warm or cold.

8 Fairy cakes and cookies

209 Reindeer cupcakes

Preparation time:
40 minutes

Cooking time:
13–15 minutes

Oven temperature:
180°C (350°F), Gas Mark 4

Makes:
12 cakes

1 tablespoon cocoa powder
1 tablespoon boiling water
125 g (4 oz) unsalted butter, softened
2 eggs
125 g (4 oz) caster sugar
125 g (4 oz) self-raising flour

TO DECORATE:
**150 g (5 oz) plain dark chocolate,
  chopped**
1 tablespoon cocoa powder
1 tablespoon boiling water
50 g (2 oz) unsalted butter, softened
125 g (4 oz) icing sugar
6 glacé cherries
**1 small packet of candy-coated
  chocolate sweets**

Put the cocoa powder in a bowl and mix to a smooth paste with the boiling water. Put all the remaining cake ingredients in a bowl and beat until smooth. Stir in the cocoa paste.

Line a 12-section bun tin with paper cases and spoon in the mixture. Bake the cakes in a preheated oven, 180°C (350°F), Gas Mark 4, for 13–15 minutes or until they are well risen. Leave to cool.

Meanwhile, put the chocolate in a heatproof bowl and melt over a saucepan of gently simmering water. Spoon into a piping bag and pipe lines about 6 cm (2¹/₂ inches) long on a baking tray lined with nonstick baking paper. Pipe small branches for antlers. Make enough for 2 for each cake with extras in case of breakages. Leave to dry and harden.

Mix the cocoa powder with the boiling water in a large bowl. Add the butter then gradually beat in the icing sugar. Spread the icing over the tops of the cakes. Add a halved cherry for a nose and 2 little sweets for eyes, piping on the remaining melted chocolate to make eyeballs. Peel the antlers off the baking paper and stick at angles into the cakes.

210 Vanilla fairy cakes

Preparation time:
10 minutes

Cooking time:
18–20 minutes

Oven temperature:
180°C (350°F), Gas Mark 4

Makes:
12 cakes

150 g (5 oz) unsalted butter, softened
150 g (5 oz) caster sugar
175 g (6 oz) self-raising flour
3 eggs
1 teaspoon vanilla extract

Put all the cake ingredients in a mixing bowl and beat until the mixture is light and creamy.

Line a 12-section bun tin with paper cake cases and spoon the mixture into the paper cases. Bake in a preheated oven, 180°C (350°F), Gas Mark 4, for 18–20 minutes or until risen and just firm to the touch. Transfer to a wire rack to cool.

COOK'S NOTES To make chocolate fairy cakes substite 15 g (¹/₂ oz) cocoa powder for 15 g (¹/₂ oz) of the flour, or add a handfull of rasins for a fruity alternative.

211 Snow-covered ginger muffins

212 Carrot cupcakes

Preparation time:
30 minutes, plus setting

Cooking time:
15–20 minutes

Oven temperature:
180°C (350°F), Gas Mark 4

Makes:
12 muffins

125 g (4 oz) unsalted butter
125 ml (4 fl oz) maple syrup
125 g (4 oz) light muscovado sugar
225 g (7½ oz) self-raising flour
1 teaspoon baking powder
1 teaspoon ground ginger
2 eggs
125 ml (4 fl oz) milk
3 tablespoons glacé ginger, chopped,
    plus extra to decorate

ICING:
200 g (7 oz) icing sugar, sifted
4 teaspoons water
2 pieces of glacé ginger, sliced

Put the butter, syrup and sugar in a saucepan and heat gently, stirring, until the butter has melted. Remove from the heat. Mix the flour, baking powder and ground ginger together in a bowl. Beat the eggs and milk in another bowl.

Beat the butter mixture into the flour, then gradually beat in the egg and milk mixture. Stir in the glacé ginger.

Line a 12-section muffin tin with paper muffin cases and spoon the mixture into the paper cases. Bake in a preheated oven, 180°C (350°F), Gas Mark 4, for 10–15 minutes or until well risen and cracked. Leave to cool.

Meanwhile, sift the icing sugar into a bowl and gradually mix in the water to create a smooth, spoonable icing. Drizzle random lines of icing from a spoon over the muffins and complete with slices of ginger. Leave to harden for 30 minutes before serving.

Preparation time:
15 minutes

Cooking time:
25 minutes

Oven temperature:
180°C (350°F), Gas Mark 4

Makes:
12 cakes

125 g (4 oz) unsalted butter, softened
125 g (4 oz) light muscovado sugar
150 g (5 oz) self-raising flour
1 teaspoon baking powder
1 teaspoon ground mixed spice
75 g (3 oz) ground almonds
2 eggs
finely grated rind of ½ orange
150 g (5 oz) carrots, grated
50 g (2 oz) sultanas

Put the butter, sugar, flour, baking powder, mixed spice, ground almonds, eggs and orange rind in a mixing bowl and beat until the mixture is light and creamy. Add the grated carrots and sultanas and stir in until evenly combined.

Line a 12-section bun tin with paper cake cases and spoon the mixture into the paper cases. Bake in a preheated oven, 180°C (350°F), Gas Mark 4, for 25 minutes or until risen and just firm to the touch. Leave to cool in the bun tin.

COOK'S NOTES Make banana-flavoured cakes by replacing the grated carrots and orange rind with 1 large banana, mashed until it is smooth.

213 Fruit and nut fairy cakes

214 Chocolate fudge fairy cakes

Preparation time:	150 g (5 oz) unsalted butter, softened
10 minutes	**150 g (5 oz) light muscovado sugar**
	200 g (7 oz) self-raising flour
Cooking time:	**3 eggs**
25 minutes	**1 teaspoon almond extract**
	50 g (2 oz) chopped mixed nuts
Oven temperature:	**75 g (3 oz) mixed dried fruit**
180°C (350°F), Gas Mark 4	

Makes:
12 cakes

Put the butter, sugar, flour, eggs and almond extract in a mixing bowl and beat until the mixture is light and creamy. Add the chopped nuts and dried fruit and stir in until evenly combined.

Line a 12-section bun tin with paper cake cases and spoon the mixture into the paper cases. Bake in a preheated oven, 180°C (350°F), Gas Mark 4, for 25 minutes or until risen and just firm to the touch. Transfer to a wire rack to cool.

Preparation time:	100 g (3½ oz) plain dark or milk
5 minutes	**chocolate, chopped**
	2 tablespoons milk
Cooking time:	**50 g (2 oz) unsalted butter**
5 minutes	**75 g (3 oz) icing sugar**
	12 Fairy Cakes (see recipe 210)
Makes:	
12 cakes	

Put the chocolate, milk and butter in a small, heavy-based saucepan and heat gently, stirring, until the chocolate and butter have melted.

Remove from the heat and stir in the icing sugar until smooth. Spread the icing over the tops of the fairy cakes while they are still warm.

COOK'S NOTES This quick and easy recipe for chocolate fudge icing can be used on larger cakes if you wish. Always use good-quality chocolate containing a high percentage of chocolate fats.

215 Snakes in the jungle

216 Ladybirds

Preparation time:
45 minutes

Makes:
12 cakes

**2 tablespoons strawberry or raspberry
  jam
12 Fairy Cakes (see recipe 210)
175 g (6 oz) green ready-to-roll icing
4 flaked chocolate bars, cut into 5 cm
  (2 inch) lengths
50 g (2 oz) red ready-to-roll icing
50 g (2 oz) yellow ready-to-roll icing
50 g (2 oz) white ready-to-roll icing
25 g (1 oz) black ready-to-roll icing**

Brush jam over the top of each cake. Knead the green icing, roll it out thinly and cut out 12 circles, each 6 cm (2¹/₂ inch) across, and put a circle on top of each cake.

Take a small ball, about 7 g (¹/₄ oz), of coloured icing and roll under the palm of you hand to make a thin sausage, 12–15 cm (5–6 inches) long, tapering it to a point at one end and shaping a head at the other. Flatten the head slightly and mark a mouth with a knife.

Thinly roll a little icing in a contrasting colour and cut out small diamond shapes. Use a damp paintbrush to secure these along the snake. Wrap the snake around a length of flaked chocolate and position on top of a cake.

Make more snakes in the same way, kneading small amounts of the coloured icing together to make different shades. For some of the cakes, press the chocolate bar vertically into the cake.

Make the snakes' eyes by rolling small balls of white icing and pressing tiny balls of black icing over them. Secure to the snake heads with a damp paintbrush.

Preparation time:
30 minutes

Makes:
12 cakes

**2 tablespoons raspberry or strawberry
  jam
12 Fairy Cakes (see recipe 210)
175 g (6 oz) red ready-to-roll icing
125 g (4 oz) black ready-to-roll icing
15 g (¹/₂ oz) white ready-to-roll icing
small piece of candied orange peel, cut
  into matchstick lengths**

Brush jam over the top of each cake. Knead the red icing, roll it out thinly and cut out 12 circles, each 6 cm (2¹/₂ inches) across, and put a circle on top of each cake.

Roll out thin strips of black icing and position one across each red circle, securing with a damp paintbrush. Roll out half the remaining black icing to a thin sausage shape, about 1 cm (¹/₂ inch) in diameter. Cut the sausage into thin slices and secure to the cakes to represent ladybird spots.

From the remaining black icing make oval-shaped heads and secure in place. Roll small balls of the white icing for eyes and press tiny balls of black icing over them. Secure with a damp paintbrush.

Make the ladybirds' antennae by pressing the candied peel into position behind the heads and pressing small balls of black icing on to their ends. Use tiny pieces of white icing to shape smiling mouths.

COOK'S NOTES Thin strips of candied orange peel are used for the antennae on these little insects. If you cannot get candied orange peel use small chocolate sticks instead.

Preparation time: **45 minutes**	**¹/₂ quantity Buttercream (see recipe 218)** **12 Fairy Cakes (see recipe 210)** **100 g (3¹/₂ oz) brown ready-to-roll icing**
Makes: **12 cakes**	**100 g (3¹/₂ oz) yellow ready-to-roll icing** **100 g (3¹/₂ oz) pink ready-to-roll icing** **15 g (¹/₂ oz) white ready-to-roll icing** **15 g (¹/₂ oz) black ready-to-roll icing** **black food colouring**

Spread a thick layer of buttercream over 4 of the cakes and lightly peak. Spread the rest of the buttercream over the remaining cakes.

Make the sheep from 75 g (3 oz) of the brown icing; wrap the remainder in clingfilm. Knead the icing. Reserve a small piece for the ears and roll the rest into 4 balls. Flatten each into an oval and gently press on to the cakes thickly spread with buttercream. Shape and position small ears on each sheep.

Make the cows from yellow icing. Reserve a small piece for the ears and roll the rest into 4 balls. Flatten each into an oval as large as the top of the cakes. Gently press on to 4 more cakes. Shape and position the ears. Use the remaining brown icing to shape the cows' nostrils and horns, securing with a damp paintbrush.

Make the pigs from pink icing. Reserve 25 g (1 oz) for the snouts and ears and roll the rest into 4 balls and flatten into rounds, almost as large as each cake top. Shape and position the snouts and floppy ears, pressing 2 holes in each snout with a cocktail stick or fine skewer.

Use the white and black icing to make all the animals' eyes. Roll small balls of white icing and press tiny balls of black icing over them. Secure with a damp paintbrush. Use a fine paintbrush, dipped in black food colouring, to paint on additional features.

Preparation time: **25 minutes**	**pink food colouring** **12 Fairy Cakes (see recipe 210)** **edible silver balls**
Makes: **12 cakes**	BUTTERCREAM: **100 g (3¹/₂ oz) unsalted butter, softened** **150 g (5 oz) icing sugar**

Make the buttercream. Beat the butter in a bowl with a little of the sugar until smooth. Add the remaining sugar and beat until pale and fluffy. Add a few drops of boiling water and beat for a little longer.

Divide the buttercream between 2 bowls and add a few drops of pink food colouring to one bowl. Mix well to colour and spread the pink buttercream over the tops of the fairy cakes to within 5 mm (¹/₄ inch) of the edges, doming it up slightly in the centre.

Put half the white buttercream in a piping bag fitted with a writing nozzle and the remainder in a bag fitted with a star nozzle. Pipe lines, 1 cm (¹/₂ inch) apart, across the pink buttercream, then in the other direction to make a diamond pattern.

Use the icing in the other bag to pipe stars around the edges. Decorate the piped lines with silver balls.

COOK'S NOTES The best buttercream is soft and fluffy with a flavour that's not too overpoweringly sweet. The quantity above is enough to sandwich and spread over the top of an 18–20 cm (7–8 inch) cake or to cover the top and sides. Make chocolate buttercream by dissolving 2 tablespoons cocoa powder in 2 tablespoons water and beating it into the buttercream.

219 Number cakes

Preparation time: **15 minutes**	**1 quantity Buttercream (see recipe 218)** **green or yellow food colouring** **12 Fairy Cakes (see recipe 210)**
Makes: **12 cakes**	**175 g (6 oz) white ready-to-roll icing** **50 g (2 oz) red ready-to-roll icing** **50 g (2 oz) blue ready-to-roll icing** **coloured sugar strands**

Colour the buttercream with green or yellow food colouring and spread all over the tops of the fairy cakes.

Knead the white icing, roll it out and cut out 12 circles, each 6 cm (2¹/₂ inches) across. Gently press one on to the top of each cake.

Roll out the red icing and cut out half the numbers. Secure to the cakes with a damp paintbrush. Use the blue icing for the remaining numbers.

Lightly brush the edges of white icing with a damp paintbrush and scatter over the sugar strands.

220 Christmas stars

Preparation time: **25 minutes**	**100 g (3¹/₂ oz) white ready-to-roll icing** **200 g (7 oz) icing sugar, plus extra for** **dusting**
Makes: **12 cakes**	**12 Fairy Cakes (see recipe 210)** **¹/₂ quantity Buttercream (see recipe 218)** **4–5 teaspoons cold water** **25 g (1 oz) desiccated coconut**

Knead the white icing, roll it out thickly and cut out star shapes with a small biscuit cutter. Transfer the stars to a lined baking sheet and leave to harden.

Meanwhile, cut out a deep, cone-shaped centre from each cake. Fill the cavity in each cake with buttercream and position a cut-out cone on each, crust side down.

Mix the icing sugar in a bowl with the cold water until smooth. Carefully spread the icing over the cakes and scatter with desiccated coconut. Gently press a star into the top of each cake and leave to set.

COOK'S NOTES These festive cakes look stunning on the Christmas tea table. If you have time, make the stars at least 2 hours in advance so they have firmed up before you decorate the cakes.

221 Love hearts

222 Easter nests

Preparation time:	200 g (7 oz) icing sugar
20 minutes	4–5 teaspoons rosewater or lemon juice
	12 Fairy Cakes (see recipe 210)
Makes:	100 g (3½ oz) red ready-to-roll icing
12 cakes	6 tablespoons strawberry jam

Put the icing sugar in a bowl and add 4 teaspoons of the rosewater or lemon juice. Mix until smooth, adding a little more liquid if necessary, until the icing is a thick paste. Spread over the tops of the cakes.

Knead the red icing, roll it out thickly and cut out 12 heart shapes with a biscuit cutter. Place a heart on top of each cake.

Press the jam through a small sieve to remove the seeds or pulp. Put the sieved jam in a small piping bag fitted with a writing nozzle. Pipe small dots into the icing around the edges of each cake and pipe a line of jam around the edges of each heart.

Preparation time:	1 quantity Chocolate Buttercream (see recipe 218) or Chocolate Fudge Icing (see recipe 214)
20 minutes	
Makes:	12 chocolate-flavoured bought fairy cakes
12 cakes	200 g (7 oz) flaked chocolate bars, cut into 2.5 cm (1 inch) lengths
	36 candy-covered chocolate mini eggs

Spread the buttercream or icing over the tops of the cakes, spreading the mixture right to the edges.

Cut the lengths of flaked chocolate bars lengthways into thin shards. Arrange the shards around the edges of the cakes, pressing them into the icing at different angles to resemble birds' nests. Pile 3 eggs into the centre of each 'nest'.

COOK'S NOTES Make these as a family treat for Valentine's Day. Use Chocolate Fudge Icing (see recipe 214) made with white chocolate instead of the glacé icing if you prefer.

223 Ducks, bunnies and chicks

224 Flying bats

Preparation time:
25 minutes

Makes:
12 cakes

1 quantity Buttercream (see recipe 218)
yellow and blue food colourings
12 Fairy Cakes (see recipe 210)
2 glacé cherries

Preparation time:
30 minutes

Makes:
12 cakes

125 g (4 oz) black ready-to-roll icing
2 tablespoons clear honey
12 Fairy Cakes (see recipe 210)
175 g (6 oz) orange ready-to-roll icing
1 tube black writing icing
selection of tiny red, orange and yellow sweets

Put two-thirds of the buttercream in a bowl, beat in a few drops of yellow food colouring and mix well. Spread the yellow icing in a flat layer over the tops of the cakes.

Colour the remaining buttercream with blue food colouring. Place in a piping bag fitted with a writing nozzle and pipe simple duck, bunny and chick shapes on to the iced cakes. Cut the glacé cherries into thin slices, then into tiny triangles and use them to represent beaks on the ducks and chicks and tiny eyes on the bunnies.

Knead the black icing, roll it out thickly and cut out 12 bat shapes by hand or using a small biscuit cutter. Transfer to a lined baking sheet and leave to harden.

Meanwhile, spread 1/2 teaspoon honey over the top of each cake. Thinly roll out the orange icing and cut out 12 circles, each 6 cm (2 1/2 inches) across. Place an orange circle on top of each cake.

Place a bat on top of each cake and pipe a wiggly line of black icing around the edges. Dampen the edge of the orange icing and press the sweets gently into the icing.

COOK'S NOTES These cute cakes will delight younger children. Why not try different combinations of colouring and shapes to suit the occasion – the possibilities are endless!

225 Butterfly cakes

226 Pied piper cakes

Preparation time:	**12 Fairy Cakes (see recipe 210)**
15 minutes	**1 quantity Buttercream (see recipe 218)**
Makes:	
12 cakes	

Cut out the centre from each cake and slice each scooped-out piece of cake in half.

Put the buttercream in a big piping bag fitted with a large star nozzle. Pipe a large swirl of icing into the hollow of each cake.

Reposition the cut-out centres on each cake at an angle of 45 degrees so they resemble butterfly wings.

Preparation time:	**200 g (7 oz) icing sugar, plus a little extra**
30 minutes	**1–2 tablespoons lemon or orange juice**
	12 Fairy Cakes (see recipe 210)
Makes:	**½ quantity Buttercream (see recipe 218)**
12 cakes	**pink and lilac food colourings**

Mix the icing sugar in a bowl with 1 tablespoon of the lemon or orange juice. Gradually add the remaining juice, stirring well, until the icing holds its shape but is not difficult to spread. You might not need to use all the juice.

Reserve 3 tablespoons of the icing and spread the rest over the tops of the cakes. Stir a little extra icing sugar into the reserved icing to thicken it until it just forms peaks when lifted with a knife. Put in a piping bag fitted with a writing nozzle.

Colour half the buttercream with pink food colouring and the other half with lilac. Place in separate piping bags fitted with star nozzles. Pipe rows of pink, lilac and white icing across some of the cakes.

COOK'S NOTES These cakes are great fun for all the family to create – children love piping their own designs and personalizing cakes with names or messages. The pink and lilac piping looks pretty on the white background, but you can choose any mixture of colours you like.

227 Stars, spots and stripes

228 Chocolate toffee fairy cakes

Preparation time:	½ **quantity Buttercream (see recipe 218)**
20 minutes	**12 Fairy Cakes (see recipe 210)**
	150 g (5 oz) white ready-to-roll icing
Makes:	**125 g (4 oz) blue ready-to-roll icing**
12 cakes	

Spread the buttercream in a thin layer over the tops of the cakes.

Knead the icings, keeping the colours separate. Roll out 50 g (2 oz) of the white icing and cut out 4 circles, each 6 cm (2½ inches) across. Cut out 6 small stars from each circle using a tiny star-shaped cutter. Thinly roll out a little of the blue icing and cut out stars. Fit the blue stars into each white round and carefully transfer to 4 of the cakes.

Thinly roll out another 50 g (2 oz) of the white icing. Roll small balls of blue icing between your finger and thumb. Press at intervals on to the white icing. Gently roll with a rolling pin so the blue icing forms dots over the white. Cut out 4 circles using a round biscuit cutter and transfer to 4 more of the cakes.

From the remaining blue and white icing cut out strips, 5 mm (¼ inch) wide, and lay them on the work surface to make stripes. Roll lightly with a rolling pin to flatten and secure them, then cut out 4 more circles. Place them on top of the remaining 4 cakes.

Preparation time:	**200 g (7 oz) can sweetened condensed**
20 minutes	**milk**
	50 g (2 oz) caster sugar
Cooking time:	**65 g (2½ oz) unsalted butter**
5 minutes	**2 tablespoons golden syrup**
	12 Fairy Cakes (see recipe 210)
Makes:	**100 g (3½ oz) plain dark chocolate,**
12 cakes	**chopped**
	100 g (3½ oz) milk chocolate, chopped

Put the condensed milk, sugar, butter and golden syrup in a heavy-based saucepan and heat gently, stirring, until the sugar dissolves. Cook over a gentle heat, stirring, for about 5 minutes until the mixture has turned a pale fudge colour. Leave to cool for 2 minutes then spoon the toffee over the top of the cakes.

Melt the plain and milk chocolates in separate heatproof bowls, either one at a time in the microwave or by resting each bowl over a saucepan of gently simmering water. Place a couple of teaspoons of each type of melted chocolate on a cake, mixing up the colours. Tap the cake on the work surface to level the chocolate.

Use the tip of a cocktail stick or fine skewer to swirl the chocolates together to marble them lightly. Repeat on the remaining cakes.

COOK'S NOTES Most children can't resist chocolate and these cakes are sure to be a favourite. Great for a party tea or tea-time treat.

229 Lantern cakes

230 Ginger snowmen

Preparation time:
40 minutes, plus drying

Makes:
4 cakes

7 g (¹/₄ oz) sachet dried egg white
4 tablespoons warm water
2 tablespoons liquid glucose
500 g (1 lb) icing sugar, sifted
yellow and red paste food colouring
4 American-style muffins
4 tablespoons apricot jam, sieved
cornflour, for dusting

Put the dried egg white in a large bowl and gradually mix to a thin smooth paste with the water. Add the liquid glucose and then gradually beat in the icing sugar with a wooden spoon, using your hands when it becomes too stiff to stir, to make a smooth, soft, rollable icing.

Colour 50 g (2 oz) of the icing yellow and wrap it in clingfilm until required. Colour the remainder orange using yellow and red food colourings. Spread the tops and sides of the muffins with the sieved jam, reserving a little.

Cut the orange icing into 4 and roll each piece piece on a surface dusted with cornflour to make a circle large enough to encase a muffin. Wrap the icing around the muffin to cover it completely. Trim off any excess. Cover the other 3 muffins in the same way.

Roll out the yellow icing and cut out jagged mouth shapes and triangles for eyes. Stick to the side of the icing-covered cakes with a little jam. Roll trimmings of both colours into a short fat 'rope' and score with a knife. Cut the 'rope' into short lengths and stick them on top of each cake for pumpkin stalks. Leave to dry for 2–3 hours or overnight.

COOK'S NOTES Great for Halloween or as a spooky treat for parties, these fun cakes are sure to delight.

Preparation time:
30 minutes, plus drying

Cooking time:
7–8 minutes

Oven temperature:
180°C (350°F), Gas Mark 4

Makes:
12 biscuits

150 g (5 oz) plain flour
50 g (2 oz) caster sugar
1 teaspoon ground ginger
100 g (3¹/₂ oz) unsalted butter, cut into
   pieces
24 small coloured balls or tiny sweets
125 g (4 oz) ready-to-roll white icing
pink and blue food colouring
small tube black writing icing

ICING:
125 g (4 oz) icing sugar
1 pinch of ground ginger
5 teaspoons water

Put the flour, sugar and ginger in a bowl, add the butter and rub in with your fingertips until the mixture resembles fine breadcrumbs. Form the dough into a soft ball with your hands. Knead lightly, then roll out thinly between 2 pieces of nonstick baking paper.

Use a 10 cm (4 inch) biscuit cutter to cut out snowmen shapes. Transfer them to ungreased baking sheets and bake in a preheated oven, 180°C (350°F), Gas Mark 4, for 7–8 minutes or until pale golden. Leave to cool on the baking sheets then transfer to a wire rack set over the sheets.

Make the icing. Sift the icing sugar and ginger into a bowl and gradually mix in the water until smooth. Spoon over the biscuits and allow to drizzle over the edges. Position the silver balls for eyes, then leave to dry and harden.

Colour half the ready-to-roll icing pink and the other half blue. Roll out on a surface dusted with a little icing sugar and cut out strips for scarves. Drape the scarves around the snowmen's necks. Re-roll the trimmings and cut semicircles for the hats and shape small balls for the pompoms. Add to the snowmen, sticking on the pompoms with a little water. Pipe on small, black, smiling mouths. Leave for 1 hour to harden before serving.

Preparation time:	75 g (3 oz) unsalted butter
40 minutes	4 tablespoons golden syrup
	100 g (3¹/₂ oz) caster sugar
Cooking time:	1 teaspoon ground cinnamon
15–17 minutes	¹/₂ teaspoon ground ginger
	1 large pinch of ground allspice
Oven temperature:	300 g (10 oz) plain flour
180°C (350°F), Gas Mark 4	1 teaspoon bicarbonate of soda
	3 tablespoons milk
Makes:	125 g (4 oz) ready-to-pipe white icing
25 biscuits	a few edible coloured balls (optional)

Preparation time:	225 g (7¹/₂ oz) plain flour
35 minutes	75 g (3 oz) caster sugar
	150 g (5 oz) unsalted butter, cut into
Cooking time:	pieces
16 minutes	50 g (2 oz) hazelnuts, finely ground
	finely grated rind of ¹/₂ lemon
Oven temperature:	1 egg yolk
160°C (325°F), Gas Mark 3	4 tablespoons seedless raspberry jam
	icing sugar, to dust
Makes:	
16 biscuits	

Put the butter, syrup and sugar in a saucepan and heat gently, stirring occasionally, until the butter has melted and the sugar has dissolved. Take the pan off the heat and stir in the spices. Mix together the flour and bicarbonate of soda and beat into the spicy butter mixture, adding enough milk to make a smooth dough.

Turn out the dough on a lightly floured surface, and when it is cool enough to handle knead it well and roll it out. Cut out festive shapes using star, stocking, reindeer, Santa and bell-shaped biscuit cutters. Re-roll the trimmings and cut out more shapes. Transfer the shapes to lightly oiled baking sheets.

Make a hole in the top of each biscuit with the end of a skewer and bake in a preheated oven, 180°C (350°F), Gas Mark 4, for 10–12 minutes or until browned. Enlarge the hole for ribbon if needed. Allow to cool on the baking sheets.

Pipe the icing on the biscuits, add the coloured balls (if used) and leave to set. Thread fine ribbons through the holes on the biscuits and tie them to the Christmas tree. Eat within 2 days.

Put the flour and sugar into a mixing bowl or a food processor, add the butter and rub in with your fingertips until the mixture resembles fine breadcrumbs. Stir in the ground hazelnuts and lemon rind, then mix in the egg yolk and form the mixture into a firm dough using your hands.

Turn out the dough on a lightly floured surface and knead it. Roll out half the dough to 1 cm (¹/₂ inch) thick and cut out rounds, 6 cm (2¹/₂ inches) across, with a fluted cutter. Arrange these on an ungreased baking sheet. Use a biscuit cutter to remove 2.5 cm (1 inch) hearts and stars from the centres of half of the biscuits. Bake the first batch in a preheated oven, 160°C (350°F), Gas Mark 3, for about 8 minutes, until pale golden-brown.

Meanwhile, roll out the second half of the dough and cut shapes as before. Re-roll the trimmings, cutting out shapes until all the dough has been used, and bake as before. Leave the biscuits on the baking sheets for 1–2 minutes to harden, then transfer to a wire rack to cool.

Spoon the jam into the centres of the whole biscuits and spread thickly, leaving a border of biscuit showing. Cover with the hole-cut biscuits, dust with a little sifted icing sugar and leave to cool completely.

COOK'S NOTES Use tiny heart- and star-shaped cutters to cut out the centres of these biscuits for a professional finish.

233 Spooky cookies

234 Chunky monkey cookies

Preparation time:
45 minutes

Cooking time:
10–12 minutes

Oven temperature:
180°C (350°F), Gas Mark 4

Makes:
20 biscuits

1 quantity Tree Decorations dough (see recipe 231)

TO DECORATE:
**7 g (¹/₄ oz) sachet dried egg white
4 tablespoons warm water
275 g (9 oz) icing sugar, sifted
black paste food colouring
1–2 teaspoons lemon or orange juice
red and black writing icing in tubes**

Preparation time:
15 minutes

Cooking time:
8–12 minutes

Oven temperature:
180°C (350°F), Gas Mark 4

Makes:
12 biscuits

**200 g (7 oz) plain flour
1 teaspoon bicarbonate of soda
125 g (4 oz) caster sugar
125 g (4 oz) unsalted butter, diced
1 egg
1 tablespoon milk
150 g (5 oz) white chocolate, roughly chopped
75 g (3 oz) glacé cherries, roughly chopped**

Turn out the dough on a lightly floured surface, and when it is cool enough to handle knead it and roll it out to 5 mm (¹/₄ inch) thick. Cut out ghost and bat shapes using biscuit cutters or by cutting around your own card templates. Transfer to a greased baking sheet.

Make a hole in the top of each cookie with the end of a skewer and bake for 10–12 minutes in a preheated oven, 180°C (350°F), Gas Mark 4, until the dough begins to darken. Enlarge the holes in the cookies if necessary and leave to cool.

Meanwhile, mix the dried egg white to a smooth, thin paste with 4 tablespoons warm water or according to the instructions on the packet. Gradually whisk in the sifted icing sugar. Colour half the icing black. Spoon 2 tablespoons into a piping bag and pipe an outline around the edge and around the holes of all the bat-shaped biscuits. Add a few drops of fruit juice to the remaining black icing and spread it inside the piped lines. Do the same with white icing over the ghost-shaped biscuits.

When the icing has hardened, pipe on facial features using black writing icing for the ghosts and red for the bats. Thread fine ribbon through the holes and hang up to serve.

Put the flour, bicarbonate of soda and sugar in a bowl and mix together. Rub in the butter with your fingertips until the mixture resembles fine breadcrumbs.

Beat together the egg and milk and add to the flour together with the chocolate and cherries.

Drop heaped dessertspoonfuls of the mixture, spaced well apart, on to lightly greased baking sheets. Bake in a preheated oven, 180°C (350°F), Gas Mark 4, for 8–12 minutes until lightly browned. Leave for 2 minutes to harden, then transfer to a wire rack.

COOK'S NOTES Change the flavourings depending on your children's favourites and what you can find in the cupboard. You could add dark chocolate instead of white or ready-to-eat dried apricots instead of the cherries. Alternatively, use sultanas and raisins to replace the white chocolate to make an all-fruit version.

235 Easter cookies

236 Helping hands

Preparation time:	250 g (8 oz) plain flour
20 minutes	25 g (1 oz) cornflour
	175 g (6 oz) unsalted butter, diced
Cooking time:	125 g (4 oz) caster sugar
10 minutes	few drops of vanilla extract
Oven temperature:	TO DECORATE:
180°C (350°F), Gas Mark 4	¹/₂ sachet dried egg white or the
	equivalent of 1 egg white
Makes:	350 g (12 oz) icing sugar, sifted
18 biscuits	1 teaspoon lemon juice
	selection of liquid or paste food
	colourings

Preparation time:	250 g (8 oz) plain flour
20 minutes	25 g (1 oz) cornflour
	75 g (3 oz) caster sugar, plus extra for
Cooking time:	sprinkling
10–12 minutes	few drops of vanilla extract
	175 g (6 oz) unsalted butter, diced
Oven temperature:	
160°C (325°F), Gas Mark 3	TO DECORATE:
	75 g (3 oz) plain dark chocolate, chopped
Makes:	100 g (3¹/₂ oz) icing sugar, sifted
20 biscuits	few ready-to-eat dried fruits, such as
	apricots and cranberries and /or small
	sweets, such as Jelly Tots

Put the flour and cornflour in a bowl. Blend in the butter with your fingertips until the mixture resembles fine breadcrumbs. Stir in the sugar and vanilla until mixed, then bring the mixture together with your hands and squeeze it into a smooth ball.

Knead the dough briefly, then roll it out on a lightly floured surface. Stamp out festive shapes with biscuit cutters and transfer to ungreased baking sheets. Re-roll the trimmings and continue cutting out and re-rolling until all the dough is used up.

Prick the biscuits with a fork and bake in a preheated oven, 180°C (350°F), Gas Mark 4, for 10 minutes or until pale golden. Leave to cool.

Make the icing. Mix the dried egg white with water according to the instructions on the packet. Gradually mix in the icing sugar and lemon juice to give a smooth consistency. Add extra water if the icing seems too thick. Divide between 2 or more bowls and colour to taste.

Spoon into piping bags and pipe outlines around the edges of the biscuits. Leave to dry, then fill in the rest of the surface with the same colour icing to create a smooth, evenly covered top. Leave to dry. Finally, pipe white icing over the top of the coloured surface to outline and make specific features.

Put the flour, cornflour and sugar in a bowl and add the vanilla extract. Add the butter and rub in using your fingertips until evenly mixed.

Bring the mixture together with your hands and knead gently to form a smooth dough. Roll out on a lightly floured surface to 5 mm (¹/₄ inch) thick. Cut out hand shapes from the dough, using card templates as a guide. Carefully lift the biscuits on to lightly greased baking sheets. Re-roll the trimmings and cut out more biscuits. Sprinkle with a little extra sugar and bake in a preheated oven, 160°C (325°F), Gas Mark 3, for 10–12 minutes or until pale golden. Leave to cool on the sheets.

Melt the chocolate in a heatproof bowl over a pan of just boiled water. Stir until smooth. In a bowl mix the icing sugar with 1 tablespoon water to a smooth, thick paste.

Spoon the chocolate and icing into separate piping bags and pipe fingernails and decorations. Add dried fruits or sweets as jewellery. Leave to harden for 1 hour. Eat on the same day.

COOK'S NOTES To make chocolate biscuits replace half the cornflour with 15 g (¹/₂ oz) sifted cocoa powder.

237 Chocolate chip vanilla cookies

238 Oat and fruit cookies

Preparation time:
15 minutes

Cooking time:
15–20 minutes

Oven temperature:
180°C (350°F), Gas Mark 4

Makes:
18–20 biscuits

125 g (4 oz) unsalted butter, softened
50 g (2 oz) caster sugar
50 g (2 oz) vanilla-flavoured sugar
1 egg
150 g (5 oz) porridge oats
150 g (5 oz) self-raising flour
250 g (8 oz) milk chocolate, chopped

Preparation time:
15 minutes

Cooking time:
20–25 minutes

Oven temperature:
180°C (350°F), Gas Mark 4

Makes:
16 biscuits

250 g (8 oz) peeled weight ripe bananas
2 egg whites, lightly beaten
150 g (5 oz) dates, pitted and chopped
140 g (4 1/2 oz) oats
75 g (3 oz) raisins

Put the butter and sugars in a bowl and mix until pale and creamy. Beat in the egg, then add the oats and flour and stir until combined. Stir in the chocolate.

Place heaped dessertspoonfuls of the mixture on lightly greased baking sheets, spacing them well apart, and flatten each one slightly with the back of a fork. Bake in a preheated oven, 180°C (350°F), Gas Mark 4, for 15–20 minutes or until they are risen and pale golden. Leave for 5 minutes to firm up slightly, then transfer to a wire rack to cool.

Roughly mash the bananas, leaving some chunks. Add the egg whites and dates and mix thoroughly. Stir in the oats and raisins. Set aside for 10 minutes.

Place teaspoons of the dough on lightly greased baking sheets and flatten with a spoon. Bake in a preheated oven, 180°C (350°F), Gas Mark 4, for 20–25 minutes or until the edges are lightly browned.

Leave the cookies to cool, then transfer to a wire rack. They can be stored in an airtight container in the refrigerator for up to 4 days.

COOK'S NOTES Once the cookies are cool, place them in a tin with freezer paper between the layers. Leave in wrapping to defrost. They will freeze for up to 6 months.

239 Cranberry and sunflower cookies

240 Orange meltaways

Preparation time:
15 minutes

Cooking time:
12–13 minutes

Oven temperature:
180°C (350°F), Gas Mark 4

Makes:
25 biscuits

4 tablespoons sunflower seeds
2 tablespoons sunflower oil
75 g (3 oz) unsalted butter, softened
125 g (4 oz) light muscovado sugar
1 egg
100 g (3½ oz) white self-raising flour
75 g (3 oz) wholemeal self-raising flour
grated rind of ½ small orange
75 g (3 oz) packet dried cranberries

Preparation time:
15 minutes

Cooking time:
10 minutes

Oven temperature:
160°C (325°F), Gas Mark 3

Makes:
12 biscuits

175 g (6 oz) butter, diced
finely grated rind of 1 small orange
4–5 tablespoons orange juice
200 g (7 oz) plain flour
150 g (5 oz) icing sugar, sifted

TO DECORATE:
few peeled pistachio nuts, finely
**   chopped**
glacé cherries, finely chopped, and
**   orange rind, finely grated**

Dry-fry the sunflower seeds in a nonstick frying pan, stirring constantly, for 2–3 minutes or until golden. Grind to a fine paste with the oil, using a spice grinder, clean coffee grinder or pestle and mortar.

Cream together the butter and sugar, gradually beat in the egg, then mix in the flours. Mix in the sunflower paste, then stir in the orange rind and cranberries.

Drop heaped teaspoonfuls of the mixture on to lightly oiled baking sheets, spacing them well apart. Bake in a preheated oven, 180°C (350°F), Gas Mark 4, for 10 minutes or until golden. Leave on the baking sheets to firm up for a few minutes, then transfer to a wire rack to cool.

Put the butter in a large bowl with the orange rind and 1 tablespoon orange juice, the flour and 50 g (2 oz) icing sugar. Beat the ingredients together until smooth and soft.

Spoon the mixture into a piping bag fitted with a large star tube and pipe rings, about 6 cm (2½ inches) across, on ungreased baking sheets. Bake in a preheated oven, 160°C (325°F), Gas Mark 3, for 10 minutes until pale golden.

Meanwhile, put the rest of the icing sugar in a small bowl and stir in 3–4 teaspoons orange juice to make a smooth, thin icing.

Transfer the cooked biscuits to a wire rack and brush the icing over the top. Sprinkle the pistachio nuts or cherries and orange rind over the biscuits and leave to cool.

COOK'S NOTES To make triple chocolate cookies omit the sunflower seed paste, orange rind and cranberries. Instead, use an extra 65 g (2½ oz) white self-raising flour and 15 g (½ oz) cocoa powder in place of the wholemeal flour. Stir in 75 g (3 oz) each plain dark and white chocolate dots at the end. Bake as above.

9 Birthday cakes

241 Animal ark

242 Man's best friend

Preparation time:
about 1¹/₂ hours

Serves: **28**

3 x 340 g (12 oz) packs of fun-size flaked chocolate bars
12 cm (5 inch) and 18 cm (7 inch) square rich chocolate cakes
triple quantity Chocolate Buttercream (see recipe 218)
25 cm (10 inch) square plate
200 g (7 oz) each pink, chocolate brown, light brown and yellow ready-to-roll icing
black food colouring

Preparation time:
about 1 hour

Serves: **24**

25 cm (10 inch) round bought or homemade Madeira cake or rich chocolate cake
triple quantity Chocolate Fudge Icing (see recipe 214)
30 cm (12 inch) round plate
425 g (14 oz) light brown ready-to-roll icing
200 g (7 oz) blue ready-to-roll icing
dark blue or black food colouring

Trim the chocolate bars to 1 cm (¹/₂ inch) longer than the cakes. Cut each cake into 3 layers and sandwich with buttercream. Place the larger cake on the plate and spread with more buttercream. Position the smaller cake on top and spread with the remaining buttercream. Cut each chocolate bar in half. Place around the sides of the cakes.

Make elephants by rolling a small ball of pink icing into an oval. Press it into the buttercream. Take a larger ball and mould a flattened pear shape, gradually elongating the thin end into a trunk. Impress lines along it with a knife. Prop it against the pink base, securing with a damp paintbrush. Shape and secure floppy ears.

Make monkeys by rolling a small ball of chocolate brown icing for the head and pressing it into the buttercream. Shape large ears and secure to the head. Secure a flattened ball of light brown icing for the snout.

Make lions by rolling a small ball of yellow icing into an oval. Press it into the buttercream. Flatten brown icing for the mane and indent the edges. Roll another ball of icing and flatten it against the mane. Position it on the yellow base. Add ears and a rope of icing for the tail.

Make bears by rolling a small ball of light brown icing into an oval. Press it into the buttercream. Roll a larger ball and position it for the head, adding 2 small, round ears. Secure a flattened ball of icing for the snout. Use icing trimmings to add paws and a fine paintbrush and black food colouring to add features to the animals' faces.

Halve the cake horizontally and sandwich the pieces together with one-third of the chocolate fudge icing. Put it on the plate and swirl the remainder of the fudge icing over the top and sides of the cake.

Shape the dog by rolling a 200 g (7 oz) ball of brown icing for the body. Flatten it slightly and put it on the centre of the cake. Roll a 175 g (6 oz) ball of icing for the head. Pinch one side to a point to make a snout. Rest the head, tilting it to one side, at one end of the 'body'. From the remaining icing shape small paws, droopy ears and a curved tail. Position the paws and ears and reserve the tail.

Knead the blue icing, thinly roll it out and cut out a 20 cm (8 inch) square. Drape the icing over the cake, fitting it first around the dog's head and draping it across the cake in loose folds. Position the tail.

Use a fine paintbrush and the blue or black food colouring to paint closed eyes, a snout and a mouth on the dog's face.

COOK'S NOTES The dog can easily be personalized to resemble your own dog by changing the colour of the icing and by painting on spots or patches as appropriate.

243 Spider's web

244 Funny clown

Preparation time:
30 minutes

Serves: **16**

**20 cm (8 inch) round bought or homemade
  Madeira cake**
**double quantity Buttercream (see recipe
  218)**
**33 x 35 cm (13–14 inch) round plate,
  preferably red or orange**
1 kg (2 lb) white ready-to-roll icing
1 tube black writing icing
black food colouring
15 g (1/2 oz) black ready-to-roll icing
1 flat liquorice bootlace
several sweet snakes or insects
orange or black candles

Preparation time:
20 minutes

Serves: **8**

1 quantity Buttercream (see recipe 218)
1 teaspoon vanilla extract
**18 cm (7 inch) bought or homemade
  Victoria sandwich cake**
23 cm (9 inch) thin round cake board
500 g (1 lb) white ready-to-roll icing
125 g (4 oz) red ready-to-roll icing
125 g (4 oz) blue ready-to-roll icing
1 yellow and black liquorice sweet
**100 g (3 1/2 oz) apple- or strawberry-
  flavoured bootlaces**
1 tube green or red writing icing

Cut the cake in half horizontally and sandwich it together with half the buttercream. Put it on the plate and spread over the remaining half.

Roll out about 875 g (1 3/4 lb) white icing to a circle, 33 cm (13 inches) across. Lay the icing over the cake and smooth it around the sides, trimming off the excess around the base.

Use the black writing icing to pipe 6 lines over the top of the cake, crossing them in the centre. Working from the centre outwards, pipe curved lines of icing to resemble a spider's web.

Roll 50 g (2 oz) of the reserved white icing into a ball, then mould it into a ghost shape. Press the shape on to the surface to make sure it stands upright, then secure it to one side of the web with a damp paintbrush. Paint the eyes and mouth with black food colouring and a fine brush.

To make the spider roll the black icing into a ball and put it on the web. Cut 8 pieces of liquorice, each 4 cm (1 1/2 inches) long, and secure 4 on either side of the 'body'. Put a few sweet snakes or insects on the web.

Roll the remaining white icing into a long, thin rope and arrange in a curvy line around the sides of the cake. Push the candles into the icing for support.

Add the vanilla extract to the buttercream and mix thoroughly. Sandwich the 2 halves of the cake layer together with a thick layer of the buttercream. Place them on the cake board and spread the top and sides of the cake and the rim of the board thinly with the buttercream. Reserve the remaining buttercream.

Knead the white icing and roll it out until it is large enough to cover the entire cake and rim of the board. Drape it over the cake and smooth it with your fingertips dusted with icing sugar or cornflour. Press it over the cake board so that it is firmly in place. Trim off the excess.

Shape a ball for the nose and a rope about 12 cm (5 inches) long from the red icing. Curve the rope and flatten with a rolling pin for the mouth. Stick the nose and mouth to the top of the cake with a little of the remaining buttercream.

Knead the blue icing and roll out thinly. Cut out a 28 x 6 cm (11 x 2 1/2 inch) rectangle and put this on the base of the cake in a wavy line, sticking it in place with dots of buttercream. Re-roll the trimmings and cut 2 eyes and a strip for the centre of the mouth. Press on to the cake.

Halve the liquorice sweet and stick it to the cake for eyeballs. For the hair, twist the bootlaces around a spoon handle or skewer, hold for 1–2 minutes, then slide off and stick them on to the cake with writing icing.

245 Scary shark

Preparation time:
1 hour

Serves: **12**

30 x 23 x 5 cm (12 x 9 x 2 inch) bought or homemade Madeira cake
28 x 23 cm (11 x 9 inch) thin oval cake board
1¹/₂ quantity Buttercream (see recipe 218), coloured red
500 g (1 lb) black ready-to-roll icing
125 g (4 oz) white ready-to-roll icing
2 yellow and black liquorice sweets
black paper
35 x 30 cm (14 x 12 inch) cake board

Place the cake up and with the short side facing you. For the head, measure 12 cm (5 inches) up from the bottom left-hand corner, repeat on the right and 19 cm (7¹/₂ inches) up in the centre, then cut between the marks in an arc. Cut a 10 cm (4 inch) deep semicircle from the remaining cake, using the uncut edge as the base, for the jaw.

Put the jaw on the cake board with the curved edge almost touching one end. Graduate the straight edge of the back of the jaw so the other cake section will sit comfortably, then place the shark's head on top, half on the jaw, to make the mouth. Fill in the gaps beneath the top cake with trimmings. Spread the mouth area thickly with buttercream. Spread the rest thinly over the top and sides of the cake.

Knead and roll out one-third of the black icing to a long strip and trim to 37.5 x 5 cm (15 x 2 inches). Lift and press around the jaw and a little over the head. Smooth in place. Roll out the remaining icing, curve one edge and press edge up to the top curved edge of the shark's head. Drape over the sides and smooth in place. Trim and keep any excess icing.

Cut triangles for teeth from the rolled white icing. Press the top teeth in place first, then the bottom teeth. Add 2 liquorice sweet eyeballs and press over 2 black eyelids. Cut 3 fins 18 cm (7 inches) long and a tail 43 cm (17 inches) long from black paper. Fold along the base of one fin and stand on the cake. Put the other 2 fins and tail on the large cake board, place the cake on top then curl the end of the tail so that it stands up.

246 Football boots

Preparation time:
30 minutes

Serves: **14**

2 x 20 cm (8 inch) bought or homemade Swiss rolls
2 tablespoons smooth apricot jam
500 g (1 lb) black ready-to-roll icing
125 g (4 oz) grey ready-to-roll icing
125 g (4 oz) white ready-to-roll icing
3 flat liquorice bootlaces
large tissue-lined shoe box
about 10 foil-wrapped chocolate footballs

Round off 2 ends of each of the Swiss rolls to make the heels. Out of the top of each cake scoop an oval, about 10 x 5 cm (4 x 2 inches) and 2 cm (³/₄ inch) deep in the centre. Make a sloping cut from the front of the scooped-out area down to the front end of each cake. Round off all the edges. Brush the jam over the cakes.

Dust your work surface with icing sugar and roll out half the black icing to a rectangle, 30 x 20 cm (12 x 8 inches). Lay the icing over one cake, pressing it down into the cavity. Ease to fit around the sides and tuck the ends under the boot. Dust your palms with icing sugar and smooth the icing. Cover the other cake with the remaining icing.

Roll out half the grey icing into 2 ovals, each 11 x 6 cm (4¹/₂ x 2¹/₂ inches), and press them into the cavities in the tops of the boots. Halve the reserved grey icing and shape 2 'shoe tongues', each about 12 cm (5 inches) long and 6 cm (2¹/₂ inches) across the top. Use a damp paintbrush to secure them in position.

Roll out the white icing and cut it into long strips about 2 cm (³/₄ inch) wide. Arrange them on the boots, rounding off the corners at the front and tucking the ends around the back.

Cut the liquorice into 14 pieces, each about 4 cm (1³/₄ inches) long, and use them for the laces, making holes in the white icing so that you can easily press in the ends. Use longer lengths of liquorice for the ends. Arrange the boots in the tissue-lined box with the footballs.

Preparation time:
50 minutes, plus drying

Serves: 20

homemade Madeira cake made in a 1.5
  litre (2¹/₂ pint) pudding basin
18 cm (7 inch) deep round Madeira cake
1¹/₂ quantity Buttercream (see recipe 218)
25 cm (10 inch) thick round cake board
750 g (1¹/₂ lb) white ready-to-roll icing
green paste food colouring
100 g (3¹/₂ oz) pink ready-to-roll icing
125 g (4 oz) purple ready-to-roll icing
selection of sweets and lollipops

Level the basin cake top, cut each cake horizontally in half and
sandwich together with buttercream. Spread the top of the round cake
with buttercream, then position it on the cake board close to the side.
Press the basin cake, trimmed top down, on top. Reserve 2 teaspoons
of the buttercream and spread the rest over the cake top and sides.

Knead the white icing until slightly softened. Shape a small piece into
2 eyes and reserve. Knead in a little green colouring until faintly
marbled. Roll out to a circle 35 cm (14 inch) across. Drape over the
cake so that it falls in folds, easing it down to the board. Leave a
space between the front folds for the mouth.

Knead and roll out the pink icing thickly. Cut out 2 feet and tuck under
the front of the green icing. Roll out the icing thinly and cut out an oval
mouth, 10 x 7 cm (4 x 3 inches). Stick on with water. Cut out 2 hands
and reserve.

Knead and roll out one-third of the purple icing into a rope 12 cm
(5 inches) long for the top lip, pinch together in 2 places, then stick on
to the mouth with a little of the reserved buttercream. Cut out an oval
12 x 7 cm (5 x 3 inches) from the purple icing, dot the lower underside
edges with buttercream and stick on to the mouth to create a pouch.

Shape the purple trimmings into 2 eyebrows and 2 eyeballs and with
the white eyes and pink hands, stick on the cake with water. Leave to
dry for at least 30 minutes, then add sweets to the mouth.

Preparation time:
30 minutes

Serves: 12

23 cm (9 inch) round bought or homemade
  Madeira cake
1 bought mini sponge roll
25 cm (10 inch) thin round cake board
  double quantity Buttercream (see
  recipe 218)
yellow paste food colouring
red paste food colouring
200 g (7 oz) bar plain dark or milk
  chocolate
150 g (5 oz) white ready-to-roll icing
2 yellow and black liquorice sweets
black paste food colouring

Trim the top of the large cake level. Put it on a board and lay the mini
sponge roll on top in the centre for the lion's nose. Make 2 inverted V cuts,
each about 5 cm (2 inches) deep and 5 cm (2 inches) apart, beneath the
nose to make the jaw. Reserve the trimmings for the ears. Round the jaw
with a small knife, then round the cheeks on either side. Transfer the cake
to the cake board. Stick the ears in place with a little buttercream.

Reserve 1 teaspoon of the buttercream. Colour the remainder orange
using a little each of the yellow and red colourings, then spread all over
the top and side of the cake.

Turn over the chocolate bar so that the smooth side is uppermost. Run a
swivel-bladed vegetable peeler over the smooth side to make curls and
press them around the top edge for the lion's mane.

Knead and roll 2 small balls of white icing, flatten and shape into thin
ovals, then press on to the face for eyes. Add the sweets for eyeballs,
sticking them in place with a little of the reserved buttercream.

Colour two-thirds of the remaining white icing deep orange, shape into
a curled tongue and press in place. Colour the remaining icing black,
shape into 2 flat rounds, then press on to the base of the nose. Add
small indentations with the end of a cocktail stick.

249 Pirate ship

250 Space rocket

Preparation time:	
30 minutes	4 x 300 g (10 oz) bought double chocolate loaf cakes
	35 x 20 cm (14 x 8 inch) thin silver cake board
Serves: **16**	double quantity Chocolate Buttercream (see recipe 218)
	2 x 150 g (5 oz) packs chocolate finger biscuits
	8 giant candy-covered chocolate drops
	7 long wooden skewers
	raffia or fine string
	selection of orange, green and black paper
	sticky tape
	selection of small plastic pirate figures
	shredded blue tissue paper

Level the tops of the cakes. Put 2 cakes on the cake board and sandwich the 2 shortest sides together with a little buttercream. Cut one-third off one of the cakes. Spread the top of the cakes with buttercream and stick the other 2 cakes on top with the small slice in the centre so that the second layer extends over the first. Cut one end to a point for the prow of the ship and put one of the off-cuts underneath to support it.

Spread the remaining buttercream over the top and sides of the cake. Stick chocolate fingers over both sides and add candy-covered chocolate drops for portholes.

Make the masts by tying 2 skewers in a cross shape with a little raffia or string. Trim the sticks if necessary. Repeat to make 2 more. Cut rectangles of paper for sails, make holes along the top edge with a hole punch and lace to the masts with raffia or string. Add a hole to the centre base of the sails and tie down to the masts. Add a triangular sail to a single stick mast. Cut black flags and tape to the top of the masts, then insert into the cake. Complete the cake with plastic pirate figures and tissue paper sea arranged on the cake board.

Preparation time:	
30 minutes	1 kg (2 lb) white ready-to-roll icing
	black paste food colouring
	30 cm (12 inch) thin round cake board
Serves: **6**	3 tablespoons smooth apricot jam
	1 ice cream cone
	350 g (11½ oz) chocolate marble cake
	6 chocolate mini Swiss rolls
	6 strawberry twists
	1 tube red writing icing
	2 flat liquorice bootlaces
	few black and white square and tube-shaped liquorice sweets
	few edible silver balls
	candles and candle-holders

Knead half of the white icing, keeping in the rest in clingfilm. Knead in some black colouring. Shape some of the grey icing into rings and balls and press on to the cake board. Brush the edges of the board with a jam. Roll out the remaining grey icing, drape it over the cake board and smooth it into place. Trim off the excess.

Trim the bottom end off the ice cream cone and stick to the end of the marble cake with jam. Spread the remaining jam over the top and sides of the cake and use it to stick the mini rolls together in a stack.

Roll out two-thirds of the reserved white icing and drape it over the marble cake and nose cone. Smooth it into place, trim off the excess and place on the board. Cover the mini rolls with the remaining icing. Smooth in place, then trim off the excess. Place it next to the rocket body.

Cut the strawberry twists in half and stick to the rocket engine and rocket with writing icing. Cut the flat liquorice bootlaces and stick on to the nose cone and body of the rocket with writing icing.

Thinly slice the black and white liquorice sweets and stick them on to the rocket with writing icing. Add piped lines and silver balls to the nose cone. Add the candles and candle-holders when ready to serve.

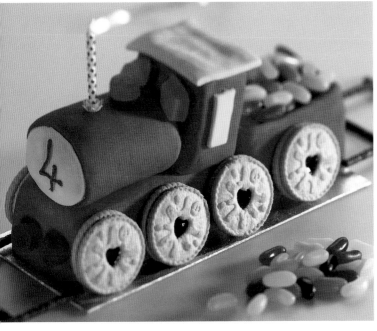

Preparation time:
30 minutes

Serves: **8**

300 g (10 oz) chocolate marble cakes
28 x 5 cm (11 x 2 inch) thin cake board
4 tablespoons smooth apricot jam
500 g (1 lb) red ready-to-roll icing
half a standard 15 cm (6 inch) jam or
  chocolate Swiss roll
75 g (3 oz) yellow ready-to-roll icing
8 round jam-filled or iced ring biscuits
1 tube red writing icing
2 large red jelly sweets
2 large yellow jelly sweets
200 g (7 oz) coloured jelly beans
1 candle and candle-holder

Level the tops of the cakes. Place one cake near the end of the cake board. Cut one-third off the remaining cake for the cab and use the rest for the tender. Spread the top and sides of all the cakes with jam.

Reserve one-third of the red icing, wrapped in clingfilm. Knead the remainder and roll out just over half. Use it to cover the engine base, smooth the surface and trim off the excess. Re-roll the trimmings and amalgamate with the remaining kneaded icing. Use to cover the cab sides and the Swiss roll boiler, leaving the ends of the Swiss roll uncovered. Place the cab and boiler in position, securing them with jam if necessary.

Cover the tender in the same way with the reserved red icing, folding the edges of the icing over the top edge of the cake. Place the tender on the cake board behind the engine.

Roll out the yellow icing and cover the cab top. Add rectangular windows and cover the end of the Swiss roll boiler.

Stick the biscuits to the sides of the engine with red writing icing. Add jelly sweet buffers and lights, sticking them in place with red writing icing and pipe a number on front of the boiler. Fill the tender with sweets and complete the engine with a candle and candle-holder.

Preparation time:
30 minutes

Serves: **6**

275 g (9 oz) bought striped angel cakes or
  plain Madeira cakes
35 cm (14 inch) oval plain or iced cake
  board
double quantity Buttercream (see recipe
  218), coloured pink
375 g (12 oz) turquoise, green or blue
  ready-to-roll icing
125 g (4 oz) pink ready-to-roll icing
1 tube each of yellow, black and red
  writing icing

Lay one of the cakes on its side. Cut it in half crossways, then shape one piece into an oval for the head. To make the other half into the body, cut triangular slices off the base for the waist and round the top corners for shoulders. Place these in position on the cake board.

Lay the second cake on its side and cut off the right-hand corner. Position the large piece at an angle to the body to make a tail, then arrange the trimmings at the end of the tail to curve slightly.

Spread the top and sides of the mermaid, including all the tail pieces, with buttercream. Knead the turquoise icing. Shape a piece into a Y, pinch the ends to a point and position at the end of the tail pieces. Roll out the remaining turquoise icing and cut out circles, 2.5 cm (1 inch) across. Starting at the base and working upwards, arrange the circles in an overlapping pattern over the tail.

Make the bikini by cutting straps from the trimmings. Complete with 2 circles. Roll a tiny ball of pink icing for the nose and position on the face. Cut the remaining pink icing in half and shape into 2 arms. Stick them on to the side of the cake.

Pipe yellow hair with writing icing and add 2 black eyes and a red mouth.

Preparation time:
30 minutes

Serves: **6**

**18 cm (7 inch) bought or homemade
   Victoria sandwich cake
20 cm (8 inch) thin square cake board
double quantity Buttercream (see recipe
   218), coloured pink
4 tablespoons strawberry jam
500 g (1 lb) white ready-to-roll icing
1 tube white piping icing
2 x 6 cm (2½ inch) thick, non-drip white
   or pink candles
20 g (¾ oz) pack of sugar flowers**

Preparation time:
30 minutes

Serves: **4**

**8 bought or homemade Fairy Cakes (see
   recipe 210)
1 quantity Buttercream (see recipe 218),
   coloured red
200 g (7 oz) strawberry-flavoured
   bootlaces
20 cm (8 inch) thin round silver cake
   board
250 g (8 oz) black ready-to-roll icing
75 g (3 oz) white ready-to-roll icing
1 tube black writing icing**

Cut a circle of paper the same size as the Victoria sandwich cake layers. Fold it into a wedge shape, retaining the curved edge. Use the folded paper as a guide to cut the cake layers into wedge shapes. Piece the trimmings together on the folded paper, trimming again where necessary, to make a third wedge.

Place one wedge on the cake board and spread thickly with buttercream so that the icing protrudes slightly over the edge. Dot with half the jam, adding some near the edges of the cake. Cover with the separate pieces of cake and spread with buttercream and jam as before, then top with the third wedge.

Spread the top and rounded side of the cake with a thin layer of buttercream. Knead the white icing and roll out to make a 28 x 25 cm (11 x 10 inch) triangle. Drape over the cake and smooth into place.

Trim the icing to the shape of the cake. Brush any crumbs off the trimmings, knead again and re-roll. Cut moon shapes about 10 cm (4 inches) long to make swags. Curl the long edges up, then drape around the side of the cake and secure with white piping icing.

Pipe rosettes of pink buttercream between the swags and around the top and bottom edges of the cake with a large star tube. Decorate the cake with the sugar flowers. Pipe larger rosettes on top of the cake and press a candle into the centre of each.

Trim the tops of the cakes to level them. Spread a little buttercream over the cake tops and sandwich them together in pairs. Spread buttercream thinly all over the tops and sides of the cakes.

Wrap the strawberry bootlaces around the cakes so they resemble balls of wool, reserving a few spare strands. Arrange the balls on the cake board and twist the remaining bootlaces between them.

Make the kittens by shaping a 3.5 cm (1½ inch) long oval of black icing with your fingers. Position it on top of, or at the base of, a cake and add a small head about 2 cm (¾ inch) in diameter. Shape 4 small legs and a tail and press them on to the body. Make ears with tiny balls of white icing wrapped in black and press them on to the kitten. Add tiny ropes of white for whiskers and stick on with dots of black writing icing. Add tiny balls of white for paws.

Repeat to make a second seated black cat in the same way, but add a circle of white icing to the tummy. Knead the remaining black and white icing together, shape into a tabby cat and arrange on a ball of wool.

COOK'S NOTES Cute and playful, these cheeky kittens will make a great addition to a bithday tea table.

Preparation time:
30 minutes

Serves: **8–10**

**2 x 15 cm (6 inch) bought or homemade
   filled Victoria sandwich cakes
1 cinnamon bagel
4 tablespoons smooth apricot jam
20 cm (8 inch) thin round cake board
500 g (1 lb) white ready-to-roll icing
250 g (8 oz) pink ready-to-roll icing
1 Barbie-style doll, clothes and legs
   removed
1 tube white piping icing
1 sugar flower
30 g (1¼ oz) pack edible mixed coloured
   balls**

Preparation time:
25 minutes

Serves: **10**

**18 cm (7 inch) bought or homemade
   Victoria sandwich cake
2 bought or homemade Fairy Cakes (see
   recipe 210) or American muffins
double quantity Buttercream (see recipe
   218)
20 cm (8 inch) oval silver cake board
125 g (4 oz) white ready-to-roll icing
red food colouring
2 candy-covered chocolate drops
1 tube black writing icing
2 packs foil-covered chocolate coins**

Stack the cakes and top with the bagel. Sandwich together with a little jam, then place on the cake board. Trim a little off the top edge of the cake where it meets the bagel to smooth the line of skirt, then spread the top and sides with jam.

Knead and roll out the white icing to a circle about 38 cm (15 inches) across. Drape the icing over the cake so that it comes down to just over the edge of the cake board. Smooth with your fingertips to make a swirled skirt shape. Trim off the excess icing and reserve.

Knead and thinly roll out the pink icing, then trim to a circle 20 cm (8 inches) across, using a knife. Cut the circle in half and drape each half around the top of the skirt, pleating and pressing it into place.

Knead the pink trimmings and roll out to a rectangle large enough to wrap around the doll. Press it on to the doll, sticking it in place with dots of jam. Trim off the excess and shape the front of the bodice. Press the doll into the cake and decorate the top of the bodice with a strip of white icing cut from re-rolled trimmings with a fluted pastry wheel.

Pipe white icing around the join of the bodice and skirt and add a sugar flower. Pipe dots over the white skirt. Add dots to the front of the dress and the ears and pipe a ring around the wrist. Press on coloured balls.

Stack the cake layers on a board and trim a little off the top and bottom to make an oval pig shape. Trim the cake on one side to make the head and snout. Trim the tops of the little cakes to level.

Spread buttercream over the top and sides of the little cakes. Place them, slightly spaced apart, on the cake board. Sandwich together the cake layers with buttercream and then spread a thin layer of the icing all over the top and sides to stick the crumbs in place. Add a second, thicker layer of icing. Carefully stand the sponge cake on the legs and spread icing over the other side. Prop up the cake with a couple of large cans to prevent it from toppling over.

Shape 2 small ovals from the white icing for eyes and stick them on to the cake. Colour the remaining icing pink with a little red colouring and shape 2 ears, a curly tail, strips to mark the money slot and a small round nose. Mark nostrils in the nose with the end of a teaspoon, then press all of these on to the cake.

Stick the chocolate drops on the eyes with a little black writing icing, then pipe on black eyelashes. Scatter foil-covered coins around the board and press one into the top of the cake. Leave until ready to serve.

257 Dinosaur

258 Smiling snowman

Preparation time:
30 minutes

Serves: **10**

**23 cm (9 inch) round bought or homemade
   Madeira cake**
6 tablespoons smooth apricot jam
**25 x 35 cm (10 x 14 inch) thin rectangular
   cake board**
500 g (1 lb) white ready-to-roll icing
**green, blue and yellow paste food
   colourings**
250 g (8 oz) red ready-to-roll icing
**50 g (2 oz) pack candy-covered chocolate
   drops**
1 tube yellow writing icing
few sugar crystals

Preparation time:
45 minutes

Serves: **12**

**2 homemade Madeira cakes made in 900
   ml (1½ pint) pudding basins**
1 quantity Buttercream (see recipe 218)
2 tablespoons apricot jam
**15 cm (6 inch) thin round cake board 1
   large, muffin, paper case removed**
15 g (½ oz) black ready-to-roll icing
25 g (1 oz) orange ready-to-roll icing
50 g (2 oz) red ready-to-roll icing
25 g (1 oz) yellow ready-to-roll icing

ROYAL ICING:
2 egg whites
500 g (1 lb) icing sugar

Cut a 4 cm (1½ inch) strip from the centre of the cake, then sandwich together the half-moon shapes with some of the jam. Stand the cake on the cake board so that the curved sides are uppermost. Halve the remaining strip of cake and use one half for the head, rounding off the corners to make the snout and back of the head. Use the other half for the tail, cutting a diagonal slice off the length of the tail piece. Turn it around and butt the pieces together to lengthen the tail. Brush the top and sides of the cake with jam.

Knead the white icing to soften it, then knead in a little green colouring until evenly coloured. Add more green, blue and yellow colourings and knead briefly for a marbled effect. Roll out until large enough to cover the dinosaur. Drape the icing over the cake, smooth the surface and trim off the excess. Cut a triangle for the end of the tail, shape legs, eyes and nostrils from the trimmings and stick them on to the cake with the remaining jam.

Knead the red icing. Shape small balls into triangles and press them along the top of the dinosaur for back spines. Roll out and cut a tongue, then press on to the mouth.

Stick the sweets on to the dinosaur's back and eye sockets with yellow writing icing, then pipe on eyeballs. Put sugar crystals on the board.

Make the royal icing. Whisk the egg whites in a large bowl with a little of the icing sugar until smooth. Gradually whisk in the remaining icing sugar until the icing is softly peaking. You might not need to use all of it. Cover with clingfilm to prevent a crust from forming.

Level the basin cake tops, and sandwich the trimmed tops together with the buttercream to make the body. Spread jam thinly all over the outside of the cakes and stand the cake upright on the cake board. Press the muffin on the body so that the domed part forms the face. Spread the muffin with the remaining jam. Spoon the royal icing over the cakes, spreading with a round-bladed knife and pulling it into peaks.

Knead the black icing and shape black eyes and buttons. Knead the orange icing and shape a tiny piece for the nose. Knead the red icing and shape a tiny rope mouth. Press these onto the snowman. Shape half the remaining red icing into a round and press on to the head for a hat. Knead the yellow icing and shape into a rope 18 cm (7 inches) long. Repeat with the remaining orange and red icing. Twist the 3 colours together, then roll out to flatten. Trim to a 36 x 2.5 cm (14 x 1 inch) strip. Make small cuts in the ends for a fringe, then wrap around the snowman as a scarf. Re-knead and roll out the trimmings, fringe one side, then roll up and add to the top of the hat for a bobble.

259 Penguin igloo

Preparation time:
30 minutes

Serves:
8

3 tablespoons smooth apricot jam
2 x 15 cm (6 inch) bought or homemade
**   filled Victoria sandwich cakes**
28 cm (11 inch) thin round cake board,
**   plain or iced**
500 g (1 lb) white ready-to-roll icing
1 bought mini Swiss roll
4 tablespoons desiccated coconut
250 g (8 oz) black ready-to-roll icing
25 g (1 oz) red ready-to-roll icing
14 edible silver balls

Spread a little jam over the top of one of the cakes and place the second cake on top. Cut away the edges of the top cake to make a domed igloo shape. Spread the top and sides of the cakes with jam and place them just off centre on the cake board.

Knead the white icing and roll out to a circle 25 cm (10 inch) across. Drape the icing over the cakes, smoothing it over the top and sides. Trim off the excess and knead the trimmings.

Cut the mini roll in half and put one piece on top of the other, sticking it in place with jam. Roll out a little of the remaining white icing and cover the mini roll, pressing a doorway shape in one end. Butt the mini roll up against the igloo with jam. Mark on snow bricks all over the igloo and tunnel entrance. Sprinkle coconut around the base.

To make the penguins shape black icing into small balls and the same number of slightly larger balls. Press the small balls on top of the larger ones. Roll the remaining black icing into 7 ropes, each about 5 cm (2 inches) long. Flatten and shape the ends into points. Wrap around the penguins' bodies for wings. Add tiny triangles of red icing for beaks and silver balls for eyes.

Shape 6–7 small white balls from the remaining white icing into ovals and then press on to the penguins' tummies. Arrange the penguins on the cake with small balls of white icing for snowballs.

260 Gluten-free clock

Preparation time:
30–40 minutes

Cooking time:
5 minutes

Makes:
20 cm (8 inch) cake

125 (4 oz) unsalted butter, softened
125 g (4 oz) golden caster sugar
2 eggs, beaten
75 g (3 oz) carrot, finely grated
125 g (4 oz) pineapple, finely chopped
2 tablespoons pineapple juice
125 g (4 oz) potato flour
50 g (2 oz) brown rice flour
50 g (2 oz) soya flour
2 teaspoons baking powder

CAROB FUDGE ICING:
50 g (2 oz) unsalted butter
3 tablespoons milk
250 g (8 oz) icing sugar, sifted
1 tablespoon carob or cocoa powder, sifted

GLACÉ ICING:
50 g (2 oz) icing sugar, sifted
about 1¹/₂ teaspoons warm water

Cream the butter and sugar in a large bowl until pale and fluffy. Gradually beat in the egg. Stir in the carrot, pineapple and pineapple juice.

Sift together the flowers and baking powder and fold into the creamed mixture. Spoon the mixture into a greased and lined 20 cm (8 inch) cake tin and bake in a preheated oven, 180°C (350°F), Gas Mark 4, for 1 hour. Turn out on a wire rack to cool.

Make the fudge icing. Melt the butter in a small, heavy-based saucepan with the milk. Add the icing sugar and carob or cocoa powder and beat until smooth. Leave until lukewarm and pour over the cake.

Make the glacé icing. Put the icing sugar in a bowl and gradually add the water, mixing until the icing is thick enough to coat the back of the spoon. Transfer the icing to a piping bag fitted with a writing nozzle and pipe on the clock numbers and hands.

Index

Note: this index is organised by recipe number

Acknowledgements

Main Photography © Octopus Publishing Group Limited/David Jordan.

Other Photography:
Octopus Publishing Group Limited/Stephen Conroy 10 bottom right, 14 left, 19 left, 19 right, 52 left, 53 left, 94 top right, 97 left, 98 left, 110 left, 111 left, 112 left, 112 right, 113 left, 116 top right, 121 left, 128 bottom right, 143 left; /Vanessa Davies 43 left, 48 right, 49 left, 49 right; /Gus Filgate 27 right, 36 left; /Jeremy Hopley 94 bottom left, 98 right, 99 left; /Vanessa Lingwood 16 right; /William Lingwood 17 right, 54 left, 54 right, 63 left, 63 right, 64 left; /Sean Myers 94 bottom right, 113 right; /Lis Parsons 6, 17 left, 31 left, 38 top left, 40 left, 40 right, 44 right, 45 right, 46 left, 62 left, 74 top left, 76 left, 76 right, 109 right, 111 right, 116 top right, 119 right, 128 top left, 128 top right, 130 left, 131 left, 140 right, 141 left, 141 right, 146 bottom right, 148 left, 148 right, 149 left, 150 left, 150 right, 151 left, 151 right, 156 right; /William Reavell 77 left, 77 right, 115 left, 123 left, 123 right, 146 bottom left, 157 right; /Gareth Sambidge 10 bottom left, 15 left, 96 left, 99 right, 128 bottom left, 130 right, 131 right, 132 left, 132 right, 133 left, 133 right, 134 left, 134 right, 135 left, 135 right, 136 left, 136 right, 137 left, 137 top, 138 left, 138 right, 139 left, 139 right, 144 left; /Roger Stowell 28 left; /Ian Wallace 10 top right, 12 left, 94 top left, 97 right; /Philip Webb 10 top left, 18 right, 22 top left, 24 left, 24 right, 25 left, 25 right, 26 left, 60 left, 61 left, 118 left.

Executive Editor Nicola Hill
Editor Emma Pattison
Design Manager Tokiko Morishima
Designer Janis Utton
Senior Production Controller Manjit Sihra
Picture Librarian Sophie Delpech